Fanny J. Crosby
An Autobiography

D0048922

BAKER BOOK HOUSE

Grand Rapids, Michigan 49506

Reprinted 1986 by
Baker Book House Company

Copyright © 1906 by
James H. Earle and Company
and published under the title,
Memories of Eighty Years

IBSN: 0-8010-2509-5

Second printing, January 1988

Printed in the United States of America

Fanny J. Crosby

Dedication

Go, little book, with many a prayer
Go on thy pinions light as air
The story and the life portray
Of her who sends thee forth today
Go, little book, God's goodness tell
Whose praise her soul enraptured sings
Who gave the harp she loves so well
And in her childhood tuned the strings
Go, little book, her years recall
With countless friends so richly blest
She murmurs not what'er befall
But feels the power of perfect rest
Go, little book, should some lone heart
Forget in thee one throb of pain
Shouldst thou but play this humble part
Thy author has not toiled in vain

Fanny Crosby in her eighty-sixth year

Contents

Introductory Statement

FOR those friends and acquaintances, who have expressed a wish to read the complete story of my life, from my childhood to the present time, I have undertaken the writing of this book. By including even some incidents that, in themselves, may seem trivial, I have tried to make this account a full and accurate autobiography. In modesty, however, I have also desired to render my story as simple as possible, in fact, to give a vivid picture of my work, my opinions and my aspirations, not only as a teacher but also as a writer of sacred songs; and if I have spoken with a frankness that may seem akin to egotism, I hope that I may be pardoned; for I am fully aware of the immense debt I owe to those numberless friends, only a few of whom I have been able to mention, and especially to that dear Friend of us all, who is our light and life.

Throughout the pages which follow I have availed myself of the kind assistance of several persons; and I desire to acknowledge here especially the services of the Biglow and Main Company for permission to make a few quotations from my copyrighted poems;

to J. L. B. Sunderlin, for the use of a number of articles that originally appeared in the "Albany Railroader"; to I. Allan Sankey, Hubert P. Main; Dr. William H. Doane and Mrs. Mary Upham Currier, for corrections, suggestions and stories of the hymns; to my sister, Mrs. Carrie W. Rider, for the single-hearted devotion with which she has aided me in every way she could to make this story of my life all that a loving sister would wish it to be; to my friend, Miss Eva G. Cleaveland, who has warmly seconded my sister's efforts; and to my cousin, William Losee, for pictures of my early home and its surroundings.

In the work of compiling, copying and arranging this book, I am indebted to the valuable services of H. Adelbert White. Like my old physician, Dr. J. W. G. Clements, through whose generous efforts my first book of poems was issued, he has sacrificed every other consideration and patiently devoted himself to my interest. This he has done, however, as a gift of friendship; and I realize that this book never would have been possible without his assistance.

But, if this little volume shall be the means of transmitting sunshine into any life, I am sure that all those, who have so generously given their aid, will feel abundantly rewarded. For myself, it is a rare privilege and pleasure to twine the blossoms I have been gathering in the garden of memory along the journey of life into a wreath which must forever be a token of fellowship and good will.

I

Flowers That Never Fade

Many of the flowers I planted in the garden of memory during a happy childhood are still blooming sweet and fair after a lapse of more than eighty years. Those that are somewhat faded, because they have not recently been watered, and those which have been crushed in the press of a long and busy life, I will try to revive until I have finished the life story that I am about to tell. Amid

> Giant rocks and hills majestic,
> Sunny glade and fertile plain,

as one of my own poems describes the surroundings among which I was reared, these blossoms of expectant youth, some of them frail promises of future harvests, were gathered in the good old town of Southeast, Putnam County, New York. In that re-

gion the traveler, perhaps to a greater degree than
the inhabitant, remembers the country as one of
wonderful wildness and grandeur. The scenery is
sublime because natural; and more majestic than
any handiwork designed by man. During the summer months the neighboring hills are studded with
great masses of foliage; and this here and there is
touched with small masses of gold and brown; and
in winter the same landscape is covered over with
spread of virgin snow. These gracious gifts of natural scenery left their own indelible imprint upon
my mind; for, although I was deprived of sight at the
age of six weeks, my imagination was still receptive
to all the influences around me; and the surround-
ing country, in its native beauty, was real enough to
me; in one sense, was as real to my mind as to the
minds of my little companions. At least the inner
meaning of all the objects that they could see with
their physical vision, to my mental sight by imagination was made somewhat more plain than may be
supposed.

Near the humble cottage in which I lived for the
first few years of my childhood ran a tiny brook,
one of the branches of the Croton River; and the
music of its waters was so sweet in my ears that I
fancied it was not to be surpassed by any of the
grand melodies in the great world beyond our little
valley. During pleasant summer days I used to sit on
a large rock, over which a grapevine and an apple
tree clasped hands to make a bower fit indeed for
any race of fairies, however ethereal in their tastes.
The voices of nature enchanted me; but they all

Birthplace of Fanny Crosby

spoke a familiar language. Sometimes it was the liquid note of a solitary songster at eventide in the distant woods; or the industrious hum of a bee at noon, when every creature but himself and the locusts was sleeping in the shade; or the piping of a cricket as night was drawing on; and how could I help thinking, now and then, that the fairies themselves were bringing messages directly to me? In childhood the tender language of the heart is the only familiar speech; and imagination the only artist of the beautiful that seems to satisfy the childish soul. In these later years, therefore, I sometimes drink from the springs whose waters were once so cool and inspiring, and then I often think that I have indeed discovered the fountain of perpetual youth, flowing from the heart of nature.

Of the family of my father, John Crosby, we have unfortunately little record; and of him I have no recollection, for he died before I was twelve months old. My mother came of a very hardy race; earnest and devout people; noted for their longevity. She herself lived till past ninety-one; and her great-grandmother attained the goodly age of one hundred and three years, and after she was eighty-two she rode from Putnam County, New York, to Cape Cod and back again, through the half-cleared wilderness.

My mother's maiden name was also Crosby; and her line traces back to Simon and Ann Crosby, who came to Boston in 1635 and settled across the Charles River three miles from town. Simon Crosby was one of the founders of Harvard College; and his son Thomas Crosby graduated from that institution in 1653.

My great-grandfather, Isaac Crosby, was noted for his wit. While in the Revolutionary War, wishing a furlough that he might visit his home to see a child born during his absence, he told his general that he had nineteen children at home and had never seen one of them. Of course his request was granted. He was the son of Eleazer Crosby and Patience Freeman, the grand-daughter of Elder William Brewster; and through Zachariah Paddock, another ancestor on my mother's side, we are also descended from Thomas Prence and Major John Freeman. When General Warren was killed at Bunker Hill it was a Crosby, I am told, who caught up the flag as it fell from his hands. Enoch Crosby, the spy of the Revolution, was a cousin of my grandfather's; and I have always read, with much interest, the account of him, given by Cooper in his novel, *The Spy*, where he passes under the name of Harvey Birch. This daring and brave patriot sleeps near one of the charming little lakes in Putnam County, not many miles from my own birthplace.

My grandmother was a woman of exemplary piety and from her I learned many useful and abiding lessons. She was a firm believer in prayer; and, when I was very young, taught me to believe that our Father in heaven will always give us whatever is for our good; and therefore that we should be careful not to ask him anything that is not consistent with his holy will. At evening-time she used to call me to her dear old rocking chair; then we would

kneel down together and repeat some simple petition. Many years afterward when grandmother had
departed from earth and the rocking chair had passed
into other hands, in grateful memory, I wrote a
poem entitled, "Grandma's Rocking Chair":

> There are forms that flit before me,
>   There are tones I yet recall;
> But the voice of gentle grandma
>   I remember best of all.
>
> In her loving arms she held me,
>   And beneath her patient care
> I was borne away to dreamland
>   In her dear old rocking chair.

She was always kind, though firm; and never
punished me for ordinary offenses; on the contrary,
she would talk to me very gently, and in this way
she would convince me of my fault and bring me
into a state of real and heartfelt penitence. My
playmates always knew that I was interested in
nearly every kind of childish mischief; and they
were not in the least hesitant about inviting me to
engage in any of their most daring exploits.

On one occasion grandmother slapped my hands
for some breach of good behavior. This grieved me
greatly; and at once bitter resentment sprang up in
my heart. Thinking to soothe me, a little companion called me out to play with him, but, as I went,
something within said, "Yes, I will play with you;

but I will hurt you, for grandma has hurt me." And so I threw a stone at him, but missed my aim; and the cloud soon passed and all was sunny again. Fifty years later, to my great surprise, when I was lecturing in Yonkers, New York, a man whispered in my ear, "Don't you remember David Ketcham, your early playmate?" Certainly I remembered him and we had a good laugh over the incident that I have just related; and, I am happy to say, over many others of a more pleasing character.

When I was three years of age mother moved to North Salem in the neighboring Westchester County, where we remained five years among a number of delightful Quaker families, who taught me to use what they called the "plain language," or the common speech of the Friends. One good man and I became constant companions; and often when he was going to mill he found me a very willing passenger, and sometimes an uninvited guest. But whenever I persisted in going he generally gave way after the first feeble resistance.

"No, thee ain't going with me," he would say; and I as surely replied,

"David, I tell thee I *am* going to mill with thee."

"Well, get thy bonnet and come along."

When I had exhausted all the methods of entertainment at my command, mother came to me and said,

"I think I have found something that will please you." Then she placed in my arms a tiny lamb, that had lost its mother; and the little orphan at once was received into the warmth of my affections.

Through the fields and meadows we romped when
the days were warm; occasionally I fell asleep under
a great oak tree with my pet by my side. But he
soon grew into a strange creature, quite unlike the
gentle lamb that I had first known, for he used to
throw me to the ground and tear my dress and
make me cry. For a time I forgave him, but at last he
disappeared, and not many days thereafter the family had mutton for dinner. My pet had not returned;
I knew at once what had become of him; so I
refused to eat meat that day, and slipped off into a
corner so as not to betray the tears that I could not
restrain. For many weeks I wore mourning in my
heart for him, and among those who vainly tried to
comfort me was Daniel Drew, who offered to replace
my pet from the flocks that he drove by our door,
though, much to the surprise of all my friends, I
declined his gift. I reasoned, why should I again be
deprived of a dear pet? I will have none; then there
will be no chance of it.

The old Quaker church still stands about as it did
when we worshiped there; and the remembrance of
these kind Westchester people is one of the fadeless
flowers.

I had a cousin who was fond of writing comic
poetry. In our neighborhood there lived an old lady,
named Mary Barbor, who was a trouble wherever
she went. One time she came to his father's house
to remain over Sunday, and asked that he write for
her a verse of poetry. At first he declined; but when
she persisted a long time he gave her the following:

Aunt Mary Barbor
Has had a good harbor
All through this holy Sabbath day;
Tomorrow morning
I have her take warning,
And pack up her duds and march away.

2

The Training of the Blind

Hail, holy light, offspring of heaven, first born,
And of the eternal, co-eternal being!
May I express thee unblamed, since God is Light,
So much the rather thou, celestial light,
Shine inward and the mind with all her powers
Irradiate; there plant eyes; all mist from thence
Purge and disperse, that I may see and tell
Of things invisible to mortal sight.—*Milton*

To look forth over the wide expanse of ocean and behold the white capped billows in their playful moods chasing each other as if impatient for the coming of the pure morn; or to look forth from the highest peak of some gigantic mountain in wonder and astonishment on the endless variety of scenes, arising like a magical forest in the distance—the ability to do this is a gift the full significance of

Rock where Fanny Crosby spent many happy hours

Will Losee

which thought can scarcely conceive or language picture. This gift of seeing is one that ought to inspire in the heart of him who possesses it many tender emotions of gratitude to the eternal one, who, amid the splendors that encircled his throne, lifted a mighty voice, and through the chaotic gloom that held in midnight darkness the silent deep, uttered the sublime command, "Let there be light."

It has always been my favorite theory that the blind can accomplish nearly everything that may be done by those who can see. Do not think that those who are deprived of physical vision are shut out from the best that earth has to offer her children. There are a few exceptions that instantly come to my mind. For example, through the medium of sight alone, does the astronomer mark the courses, the magnitudes and the varied motions of all the heavenly bodies; and only through the medium of the eye can the sculptor produce a beautiful statue from the rude and uncut marble. His sight must guide him in reproducing the image that is already modeled in his own mind; and so, likewise, of the painter, for he frequently pauses in his busy hours and turns his gaze toward the rich crimson clouds which fall so gracefully amid the glories of the autumnal sunset. He must try to reproduce the vision that he gets from them, and it is only through the eye that the picture of the actual cloud enters.

From attaining high rank in these fine arts the blind of necessity, are debarred; but not so from poetry and music, in which the mind gives us a true image of the reality. Almost every lad at school is able to relate stray bits of legendary lore of ancient and modern artists who have been blind. Indeed, who can forget Euclid, the blind geometrician; or Homer, the blind bard; or Milton, the author of that beautiful apostrophe to light which was quoted in the beginning of this chapter.

A great many people fancy that the blind learn music only by ear, never by note; and yet a number of musical experts have told me that their blind pupils learn as proficiently as others by the latter method. It is truly wonderful—marvelous—to what a degree the memory can be trained, not only by those who rely upon it for most of their knowledge of the external world, but by all who wish to add to their general intellectual culture.

But why should the blind be regarded as objects of pity? Darkness may indeed throw a shadow over the outer vision; but there is no cloud, however dark, that can keep the sunlight of hope from the trustful soul. One of the earliest resolves that I formed in my young and joyous heart was to leave all care to yesterday and believe that the morrow would bring forth its own peculiar joy; and, behold, when the morrow dawned, I generally have found that the human spirit can take on the rosy tints of the reddening east. Early and late I played with the children of my own age; and our elders were in the habit of remarking that Fanny Crosby was certain to be interested in any mischief that occurred. With the agility of a squirrel I used to climb trees, and ride horses as fleet as the wind, while I hung on to their manes for dear life, and climb stone fences, in every respect, just like other children. Whenever I tore my dress I managed to keep out of mother's sight until I fancied she would not notice it, which was a very rare occurrence indeed.

When I was six weeks of age a slight cold caused an inflammation of the eyes, which appeared to demand the attention of the family physician; but he not being at home, a stranger was called. He recommended the use of hot poultices, which ultimately destroyed the sense of sight. When this sad misfortune became known throughout our neighborhood, the unfortunate man thought it best to leave; and we never heard of him again. But I have not for a moment, in more than eighty-five years, felt a spark of resentment against him because I have always believed from my youth to this very moment that the good Lord, in his infinite mercy, by this means consecrated me to the work that I am still permitted to do. When I remember his mercy and lovingkindness; when I have been blessed above the common lot of mortals; and when happiness has touched the deep places of my soul,—how can I repine? And I have often thought of the passage of Scripture: "The light of the body is the eye; if, therefore, thine eye be single thy whole body shall be full of light. But if thine eye be evil, thy whole body shall be full of darkness. If, therefore, the light that is in thee be darkness, how great is that darkness!"

3

First Visit to New York

In the present era, with its many modes of rapid transit, one is quite liable to forget that most of them have come into being within less than fifty years, and I am sometimes amazed at the thought that not until after I was born did the first locomotive turn a wheel on this Western continent. When I ride in the mighty express trains that fly across the country, how marvelous it seems! But do not think that I belong to that class of people who looking back over many years, think the old times better than our own. It is only the memory of the past that I cherish and that memory thrills me with a pathos which I cannot, nor do I wish to forget. As I am writing, the horseback journeys of our old postman seem to have been but last week, so well do I remember how horse and rider used to flit across the landscape like the shuttle in an ancient loom, and I see again the tall, well-built kindly man (which the sound of his voice told me he was) when

25

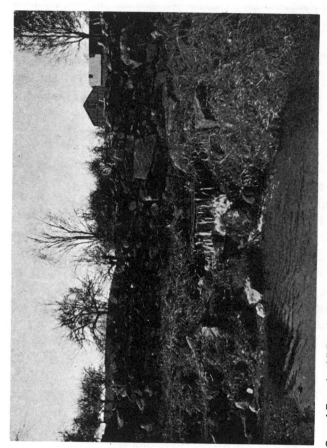

One of Fanny's childhood playgrounds

Will Losee

he came to our door the first time. We were staunch friends in a few days, for one of my household duties was to get the mail from him each Thursday. I was greatly interested to know that he had a little girl about my own age and size, and in my fond daydreams I hoped for a meeting with her some time when both of us became a little older. But I never met her, although her father continued his weekly visits for a number of years, until one morning a younger man came with the mail and announced himself as the son and successor of our old post-rider. But he did not succeed to the place in my affections occupied by his father.

A few weeks after my fifth birthday, one balmy morning in early April, mother called me to her side and said,

"We are going to New York to consult Dr. Valentine Mott regarding your eyes."

That announcement pleased me, not so much on account of the purpose of the visit, for I was contented with my lot, as the mere fact that I was to learn something of the world outside. The best that we could do in those early days was to take a sailing vessel from Sing-Sing, and a common market wagon was the only available conveyance to get us to this town. We were glad of even this, however, and so the next morning about eight o'clock we began the momentous journey. At three in the afternoon we arrived at Sing-Sing, where we went on board the vessel and one hour later the white sails began to take the wind and we were again on our way to the city at the mouth of the great Hudson River.

My mother became quite ill from the motion of the boat before we were many miles from Sing-Sing, and retired below, leaving me in charge of Captain Green and a cousin of ours who was also going down the river. To me everything about the sloop was as interesting as it was new, especially the "sea" yarns the captain told to me, and in return for his kindness, I was only too glad to sing for him the few songs that I knew. "Hail Columbia, Happy Land" was one of them; I have forgotten most of the others excepting one sad piece in which a poor wretch told a bit of his own experience. He had been convicted for beating his adopted daughter to death, and on the way to prison wrote some verses called "A Prisoner for Life." The words had no tune of their own, but I managed to find one for them among those which my friends had taught me. The first stanza is all that I remember,

Adieu, ye green fields; ye soft meadows, adieu;
Ye hills and ye mountains, I hasten from you.
No more shall my eyes with your beauty be blest,
No more shall ye soothe my sad bosom to rest.

This fragment illustrates the nondescript character of the songs that I committed to memory. One of them that I remember to this day had nearly fifty stanzas, a complete novel in verse. Some were patri-

otic; some humorous and not a few sentimental.
One ditty told the story of

> Four score and ten of us, poor old bachelors,
> Four score and ten of us, poor old bachelors,
> Four score and ten of us, and not a penny in our
>   purse,
> Something must be done for us poor old bachelors.

Whether anyone was good enough to relieve them
of their poverty I do not know, but I suspect that
they may have finally married rich widows, for their
mournful plaint has been hushed these many years.

But our sail down the Hudson was full of other
incidents, one of the best being connected with a
fellow passenger, who was taking a cow to the city;
and the cow, I am sorry to say, was better behaved
than her owner. He was somewhat under the influence of liquor; and, when Captain Green suggested
that the cow ought to be milked, he was very angry.
But at length while he was engaged in another part
of the vessel someone relieved the cow of her milk,
and my mother, who during the interval had
recovered, was commissioned to make a custard.
She did so; and even the morose owner of the cow
was obliged to pronounce her a good cook.

After what seemed to me a very long trip we
arrived at New York; but for a few days we remained
with friends in the city. I was much perplexed at
the noise, which was indeed a great contrast to the
quietness of our rural home. How well I recall every
detail of our visit to Dr. Valentine Mott. When we

arrived at his office, the famous physician was engaged with a patient, and gave me some toys for my amusement. Before I was weary of them, Dr. Mott said he was ready to make the examination, and you may be sure those were anxious moments to my dear mother. She had come what was then considered a long distance to consult the best eye specialist in America, and the result of his examination would bring her either the greatest joy or the most intense grief.

After what seemed a very long time for the consideration of my case, Dr. Mott asked me,

"Would you like to have me do something for your eyes that will make you see?"

"No, sir," I replied promptly, moving nearer to my mother, for I was afraid that might mean he would need to hurt me. After a long pause the kind physician put his hand on my head and said,

"Poor child, I am afraid you will never see again." With these words the last ray of hope died in my dear mother's heart. She knew she had done everything in her power for me and she could not help feeling sad because the object of her journey had failed, and now nothing remained for her except to return home. I could not understand why she should be so anxious concerning me. It was a beautiful afternoon in late April, for under the gentle wooing of the sun all nature was springing into life and fragrance. My sight was not totally destroyed and I could distinguish, though very faintly, any vivid color placed on the right kind of background. We had tea at five o'clock, after which I wanted to go on deck, so mother took me out and left me there while she went back and finished her supper. It was near sunset, and as there was but little air stirring the vessel rested quietly on the water. Fancy came to me and whispered that I might get a glimpse of color from the shifting waves of the Hudson.

Just as the sun was sinking slowly behind the cliffs that line the west bank the light was magnified in the mirror of the waters; and I was enabled to distinguish a few of the most brilliant of the golden hues; and as I sat there on the deck, amid the glories of departing day, the low murmur of the waves soothed my soul into a delightful peace. Their music was translated into tones that were like a human voice, and for many years their melody suggested to my imagination the call of Genius as she was struggling to be heard from her prison house in some tiny shell lying perchance on the bottom of the river. When I finally went to New York to school the noble lines of Byron became familiar; and now, whether I listen to the mighty billows of the ocean or to the smallest ripple on the bosom of some inland lake, the language of each to me is the same, and the appeal is irresistible. For

> There is a pleasure in the pathless woods,
> There is a rapture on the lonely shore,
> There is society, where none intrudes,
> By the deep sea, and music in its roar.

After the visit to Dr. Valentine Mott my life went

on as before until I was eight years old, when we moved to Ridgefield, Connecticut; and there we remained until I was fourteen. During these years my greatest anxiety centered itself in the constant thought that I would not be able to get an education; but, in the meantime, I was determined to be as content as circumstances would allow, and to hope for any good fortune that the future might have in store. To express my trust that all would be well, when I was eight or nine years old, I composed the following lines:

> Oh, what a happy soul I am,
>   Although I cannot see,
> I am resolved that in this world
>   Contented I will be.
>
> How many blessings I enjoy
>   That other people don't!
> To weep and sigh because I'm blind
>   I cannot nor I won't.

I am sure that my sentiment in these verses is more worthy than the poetic form. My dear mother at times became very sad because I was blind; and then grandmother would quote the lines of the grand old hymn of Christian faith:

> Though troubles assail and dangers affright,
> Though friends should all fail and foes all unite;
> Yet one thing assures us, whatever betide,

The Scripture assures us the Lord will provide.

When I used to hear our Presbyterian church choir sing some of the beautiful old hymns my heart was deeply moved. Seventy-five years ago there were few hymnbooks; and my earliest knowledge of sacred songs came from a tailor, who belonged to the Methodist church. All of my own friends were Presbyterians of the primitive stock; and it was not until I was twelve years old that I attended a service in the Methodist meeting house in Ridgefield. For the services in our own church it was the custom for one of the deacons to compose a hymn to be sung to some standard tune; frequently two deacons were required for a single hymn, and that not a very good one. Yet many of these homely productions possessed some genuine poetic merit. One of them I remember contained the following stanzas:

> Kind Father, condescend to bless
>   Thy sacred word to me,
> That, aided by thy heavenly grace,
>   I may remember thee.
>
> And when life's journey shall be o'er,
>   Thy glory may we see;
> Dear Savior, I will ask no more
>   Than this, remember me.

Mrs. Hawley, a kind Christian lady, in whose

house we resided, and who had no children of her
own, became deeply interested in me, and under
her supervision I acquired a thorough knowledge of
the Bible. She gave me a number of chapters each
week to learn, sometimes as many as five, if they
were short ones, and so at the end of the first
twelve months I could repeat a large portion of the
first four books of the Old Testament and the four
Gospels. At Sunday school the children would stand
in the aisles and repeat some of the passages that
they had committed during the previous week; and
there was considerable rivalry in trying to recite the
largest number. I often hunted among the records of
my memory for the longest and most involved
verses with the idea of showing my elders what a
little blind girl could do and they, in turn, flattered
me with compliments and presented me with a fine
Bible for reciting more verses than any other scholar.
Had my growing pride been unchecked by my friends
at home, it might have proven a stumbling block in
after years; and yet the habit of thoroughly learning
my lessons helped me many times when I was
obliged to commit long passages as a pupil, and
afterwards as a teacher, in the New York Institute
for the Blind.

As I have said before, our people were Calvinistic
Presbyterians, and yet the most of my friends appreciated all of the pleasures and joys of life. The good
Mrs. Hawley was kind in every respect and sought
to teach me many practical lessons that I now
remember with gratitude and affection. Of course,
the story of George Washington and his little hatch-

et was not forgotten, for it was new in those days and was emphasized even more than at present; and it was one of the mysteries of my young life how he could have been so very good while the rest of us tried so hard and often failed to attain the standard of truthfulness that the father of our country had set for us.

But I had occasion to learn my own lesson from positive experience. It happened that Mrs. Hawley had several beautiful rose bushes in her front garden; and it was understood that I might pick from any of them whenever I chose, excepting one from which grew a choice white variety. One afternoon a playmate was determined to have one of the forbidden flowers. I said, "Mrs. Hawley doesn't wish us to pick them." But my companion would not be satisfied with such a reason, and I eventually yielded and gave him one of the coveted roses. At the time Mrs. Hawley was sitting by the window and, therefore, saw the whole affair; and during the afternoon she called me to her and said, "Fanny, do you know who picked the pretty white rose from the bush yonder?" "No, madam," I answered meekly. She said no more and I thought she had forgotten the incident, when she called me to her side and read the story of Ananias and Sapphira; and, from that hour, I told no more falsehoods to my good friend.

To a young and imaginative person there is nothing more inspiring than life in the country. Existence becomes a perpetual dream of delight; and there are no pangs to sadden the buoyant spirit. The sunny hours of my childhood flowed onward as placidly as the waters of the Hudson, not many miles distant from our home. Through the secular and religious papers our town was in communication with the great world outside. To be sure, the news sometimes came several days after it had happened, but it was new to us. I used to sigh and wonder if I would ever be able to gain very much of the great store of human knowledge, but I hoped some day at least to travel and visit a few of the places of which we constantly heard. Before many years this desire for information quickened all my senses until I was eager and alert to the smallest chance of learning something. My heart sank within me, however, when I realized that there was no way for me to learn; and thus, not being satisfied, my longing for knowledge became a passion from which there was seldom any rest. A great barrier seemed to rise before me, shutting away from me some of the best things of which I dreamed in my sleeping and waking hours. I was somewhat impatient, still hopeful; but as the years succeeded each other in their usual round, what frequently seemed to me an oasis, sooner or later, faded like a mirage farther and farther into the dim and distant future.

I often went to visit my grandmother, who lived in the house where I was born; and it was a great pleasure to report the progress that I was making in the study of the Holy Scriptures. My desire for knowledge was increasing, but I found that the teacher in the village school, to which I often went with the children of my own age, was too busy to give me the personal help that I needed. Grandmother was very patient with me and did all that she possibly could for my happiness. When I went to see her she always gave me the room that I liked best; and I shall never forget one night that I spent there. Toward twilight she called me to her and both of us sat for a time talking in the old rocking chair. Then we knelt down by its side and repeated a petition to the kind Father, after which she went quietly down stairs, leaving me alone with my own thoughts. The night was beautiful. I crept toward the window; and through the branches of a giant oak that stood just outside, the soft moonlight fell upon my head like the benediction of an angel, while I knelt there and repeated over and over these simple words,

"Dear Lord, please show me how I can learn like other children."

At this moment the weight of anxiety that had burdened my heart was changed to the sweet consciousness that my prayer would be answered in due time. If I had been restless and impatient before, from that time forth I was still eager, but confident that God would point a way for me to gain the education which I craved. As I have already said, I felt no resentment against the poor physician who destroyed my eyes, but I was not content always to live in ignorance; and, in the course of time, in a way of which I had no previous intimation, my wish was to be granted in fullest measure.

4

Early Poetic Training

Even before I was eight years of age my imagination was occupied with all sorts of material that I was constantly weaving into various forms; and among these were rude snatches of verse, none of which, however, saw the light of the newspapers. My mother was in the habit of reading to me from the best poets; and I soon became so presumptuous as to believe that I could improve on some of the hymns that were composed by the deacons of our Presbyterian church. Such subjects as "The Moaning of the Wind for the Flowers" seemed especially beautiful; and some lines written on this topic were copied by a friend and sent to my grandfather, who immediately hailed me as a promising poet; but he was very careful not to say much about it in my presence, because he thought that any words of praise might blast my budding poetic genius through the pride that I might feel. Nine years from that date the same dear man walked four miles and back again for the purpose of purchasing a copy of the New York "Herald," containing some verses I had written on the death of General Harrison.

One earlier effusion, unbeknown to me, crept into the papers, and might have caused me not a little trouble. It described the dishonest acts of a miller, then living not far from Ridgefield, who was in the habit of mixing his flour with corn meal; and was sent by a friend of mine to the "Herald of Freedom," a small weekly paper published by P. T. Barnum at Danbury. The gentleman who afterward became so famous as the greatest showman in the world evidently thought my production worth exhibiting; for, much to my regret, he gave it a small corner in his paper. Thus might I have held an uncomfortable niche in the hall of fame provided by Mr. Barnum. But I chose only to exhibit the first stanza of my little ditty:

> There is a miller in our town,
> How dreadful is his case;
> I fear unless he does repent
> He'll meet with sad disgrace.

Sooner or later, I have been informed, nearly every budding poet takes to writing obituaries. My own experience at least bears out the statement; though I was among the gayest of the gay myself, the demise of any of the neighbors would cause my muse to shed a few sympathetic tears. How glad I am, however, that none of these early productions were preserved! What did' a child, full of life as I was, understand of death?

It will be more appropriate, therefore to say something about our games in Ridgefield. Every evening twelve or fourteen of us girls and boys were accustomed to gather on the common, which was directly opposite our house, and play at blind man's buff, London Bridge, hiding the thimble, or some other game that the little folks still enjoy. We had besides another one, which was named "spinning wheel," because we used to bend down the mullen plant and use it to imitate the motion of the tread of a spinning wheel, while all danced and sang an appropriate round, or some popular song of the day. One of these now remembered was "Scotland Is Burning"; and there were a score of others that have now long since passed into oblivion.

Sometimes we made a ring by joining hands and circled around a boy and a girl, who stood in the center and represented a newly married couple. Meanwhile we exhorted the boy,

> Now you're married, you must be good,
> And keep your wife in oven wood.

Some of the sentimental songs of the day were very beautiful and as well liked by the children as the modern "rag-time" ditties are by this generation. Many of them are still fresh in my mind and I

will quote a stanza from one of them. "The Rose of
Allandale" begins as follows,

> The morn was fair, the sky was clear,
>   No breath came o'er the sea,
> When Mary left her highland cot
>   And wandered forth with me.
>
> Though flowers decked the mountainside,
>   And fragrance filled the vale,
> By far the sweetest flower there
>   Was the Rose of Allandale.

Among the playmates who used to gather on the
village green was Sylvester Main, who was two or
three years older than I. He was a prime favorite with
the gentler sex, for he used to protect us from the
annoyances of more mischievous boys. In the autumn
of 1834 mother and I left Ridgefield and went to live
again in Westchester County; and I then bade my
friend, Sylvester, adieu. Not until thirty years later
did we meet again, this time, strangely enough, in the
office of William B. Bradbury with whom he was
afterwards a business partner; and from 1864 to the
time of his death in 1873 we worked together constantly.
During the winter months a music teacher came
to Ridgefield twice a week to give singing lessons.
As a text book we used the famous "Handel and
Haydn Collection," which was first published in
1832 by the celebrated Dr. Lowell Mason; and from
time to time we eagerly bought the revised editions
as they were issued. While our chorus was singing

an unfamiliar tune, "Lisbon," one evening the rest
of the singers broke down, leaving me carrying the
air all alone; and you may be sure I was much
frightened at the sound of my own voice, and would
have cried, had not the teacher spoken kind words
assuring me that I had not committed any offense. I
can still hear some of the sweet voices of my
friends reverberating through the old Presbyterian
meeting house; the tuning fork of the choirmaster
as he "set" the pitch; and the deep mellow tenor of
the minister as he answered the choir from the pulpit.

Meanwhile my imagination was always looking
for something of interest, and it was often satisfied
with romantic tales of wild life in the West, or the
story of Robin Hood and his remarkable brigands.
Some member of our household was in the habit of
reading aloud during the long winter evenings; and
many a night, when they supposed me to be asleep,
I was eagerly catching every word that was read.
"Don Quixote" interested me somewhat, but a certain story that bears the tell-tale title of "Rhinaldo
Rhinaldine, the Bandit," captivated my fancy completely; and from that winter until the present I
have always been a warm admirer of that class of
heroes—the *good* bandits of the story books. But I
have not been fortunate enough to meet any of
them in real life.

Not many months passed ere my mind was teem-
ing with sundry and diverse accounts of charitable
bandits whose habits in general were to rescue poor
wayfarers and send them on their journey with
money in their purses. For the sake of variety a few

bad robbers were sometimes thrown in; but sooner or later their chief would always emerge when they least expected it and compelled them to return their dishonest gains; and the end of the story was not reached until they repented of their mode of life and actually reformed, though, in some cases, a term in prison was necessary to settle them in their new purpose.

Another class of tales related to Sunday school children and how they went among the byways and hedges to compel the less fortunate ones to come in. One of my stories described a child left alone in the world by the death of both parents. In due time this little girl was adopted by a lady whose daughter was the wife of a sea captain, who had gone on a voyage; and just as they were sitting down to supper one evening he returned. But there was also a stranger with him, and he proved to be an uncle to the orphan girl; and though he took her home to live with him, she never forgot her former protector and friend.

Many quiet evenings I would sit alone in the twilight and repeat all the poems and passages of Scripture that I knew. Thus, ten long summers passed and I was still longing for an education, though my mother taught me many interesting things at home and read a great deal to me. It was about four years since that beautiful evening, when I knelt beside my grandmother's rocking chair and repeated over and over the humble petition, "Dear Lord, please show me how I can learn like other children."

5

The Promise of an Education

I occasionally went to school with the children of our neighborhood, and one afternoon in November, 1834, mother met me at the gate and I heard a paper rustling in her hand. My first thought was that she had a letter announcing the death or illness of some friend. Instead of that, she produced a circular from the New York Institution for the Blind, sent her by an acquaintance, in fact by the same man who had given me the little book describing the rainbow already mentioned. As she read the announcement, I clapped my hands and exclaimed,

"O, thank God, he has answered my prayer, just as I knew he would."

That was the happiest day of my life; for the dark intellectual maze in which I had been living seemed to yield to hope and the promise of the light that was about to dawn. Not that I craved physical vision, for it was mental enlightenment that I sought; and now my quest seemed almost actually rewarded.

Mother of Fanny Crosby

The New York Institution was a foreign name to me, but it was enough to know that some place existed where I might be taught; and my star of promise even then was becoming a great orb of light.

My mother was fully conscious of my joy, but to test me she said,

"What will you do without me? You have never been away from home more than two weeks at one time in your whole life."

This presented a new idea: I had not thought of the separation from her; and for a moment I wavered. Then I answered as bravely as I could,

"Much as I love you, mother, I am willing to make any sacrifice to acquire an education." And she replied,

"You are right, my child, and I am very glad you have the chance to go." But her voice betrayed the tremor in her heart. How wonderful is a mother's love.

Nearly a month before I was fifteen years old, on March 3, 1835, I made another journey to New York, one that was more pleasant and fruitful than the first had been. On the morning that I was to leave home mother wakened me from a sound sleep and told me the stage was at the door. The thought of going away thoroughly unnerved me; I dressed with trembling fingers; hastily ate a few mouthfuls of breakfast; swallowed my sobs; and then quickly hurried from the house lest I might break down completely if I waited to bid mother good-bye. You can imagine my feelings as the stage rumbled on and on toward Norwalk, where we were to take the steamboat for New York. For more than an hour I uttered not a word, although the kind lady by whom I was accompanied tried her best to cheer me and to draw me into conversation. My suffering was indeed intense, and I would have given half my kingdom at that moment, could the gift have bought me the power to shed a few tears.

Finally, my companion turned to me and said, "Fanny, if you don't want to go to New York, we will get out at the next station, and take the returning stage home. Your mother will be lonesome without you, anyway."

It was a sore temptation to return. I hesitated for a time, but, after a good cry, I felt better and said,

"No, I will go on to New York."

That decision I never for a moment regretted, for, had I returned to my mother that morning I would have cast away my pearl of great price, for it is not probable that I should ever have been brave enough to start again for the Institution.

We took the steamboat at Norwalk, and its quiet motion helped to soothe my mind after the distracting experiences of the morning; and so later in the afternoon we floated gently into the harbor of the great city, my adopted home.

For three days we remained with friends; and on Saturday morning March 7, 1835, we were driven to the New York Institution for the Blind on Ninth Avenue. There everyone treated me as though I was kith and kin to them; but I missed the companions of my childhood, the dear lady, who had accompanied me, and most of all my mother, who seemed to be far away, a thousand miles or more. When evening came they took me to the little room in which I was to sleep; everything was strange, and nothing in the place where I was accustomed to find it at home—but I bravely tried to think only of pleasant things. It was no use, however, for I could not keep the curl from coming to my upper lip; I sat there on my trunk, a forlorn being indeed, and sighed heavily. Our matron, a motherly Quaker woman, put her arms about me and said,

"Fanny, I guess thee has never been away from home before."

I replied meekly, "No, ma'am, and please excuse me, I must cry," and then burst forth the flood of tears that I had tried so hard to restrain. When the fit of weeping had passed, one of my fellow pupils came and sat down with me on the trunk; and for a whole hour we talked about everything but home.

By the next morning the worst homesickness had passed, and I was very much interested in all that was going on in the Institution. At breakfast our beloved superintendent, Dr. John D. Russ, spoke kind words of encouragement to me. Later in the day he taught a class of us children the Scripture lesson for the week; and when he had finished that, invited us to remain while he read from the poems of Lord Byron.

Our superintendent was a great benefactor of the blind. He invented the phonetic alphabet and methods of printing raised characters and maps that are used by the blind to this day. He came to the

Institution just after it was founded, and gave his services without any pay for two years. It was very difficult to make the people think that those who could not see might be educated; and Mr. Samuel Wood, who was the founder of our school, had to prove by actual tests that it could really be done. He was so successful that several wealthy men, who had before refused to help, now generously came to his aid.

Fortunately for me, our teachers read us some of the best of modern poets; and they inspired me to more determined efforts to improve whatever little gift I possessed by nature. Some of my schoolmates, however, took my crude efforts as models to be imitated; and two or three of them actually tried to compose poetry on their own account. From time to time they would make sorry work of meters and rhymes; and almost invariably, sooner or later, they would come to me for aid with the careful injunction, "You mustn't tell anyone for all the world." Thus I was sworn to secrecy; they were admitted to the poetic workshop, and actual labor began. We fitted and joined; smoothed and planed; measured and moulded, until by the joint effort of three or four people something was produced that our childish fancy took to be good verses. They were not; and years afterward all of us had many a hearty laugh over these youthful experiments.

A few of our teachers at the New York Institution were very strict with us and saw to it that no unnecessary conversation occurred between boys and girls. This we did not like—and I was one of the

first to revolt. We knew that one of the faculty of
the Institution was taking some notice of one of the
lady teachers; and to even accounts with them I
wrote the following lines:

> Say, dearest, wilt thou roam with me
>   To Scotland's bonny bowers,
> Where purest fountains gently glide,
>   And bloom the sweetest flowers.
>
> Ah, Martha, may we soon retire
>   Unto some pleasant cot,
> Where love and joy forever dwell
>   And sorrow is forgot.
>
> There in the gentle summer eve
>   We'll watch the murmuring streams;
> The moon shall fondly cheer our hearts
>   With its majestic beams.
>
> Then, let the wintry blasts appear,
>   And all the flowers decay;
> We'll sit beside the cheerful fire,
>   And sing dull care away.

Not many months after my verses were written
the unpopular teacher and his Martha did as I above
suggested, and we were rid of their unwelcome
attentions.

We used to read the Bible, *Pilgrim's Progress*,
"The Ancient Mariner" and other literary classics
in the raised letters; but our daily lessons were
received directly from our teachers, and they had an

excellent plan of instruction. Selections would be read to us two or three times, and then we were all expected to be able to answer minute questions about them in the language of the original. The following morning we were required to tell the story again, this time, however, in our own words. By this means our memory and our power of thinking were both cultivated to such an extent that I can recite verbatim most of "Brown's Grammar" as well now as the day I left school. My favorite studies were English, history, philosophy, and the small portion of science that was then taught.

In the study of arithmetic three types were used, and by placing them in a wooden frame in different positions they represented certain figures. My first lesson consisted of the multiplication tables; but you may be sure I was a very dull pupil; and two days after this assignment, Dr. Russ came in and said to the girl who was appointed to instruct me,

"Well, Anna, has your pupil learned the multiplication tables yet?"

"Not quite," she replied.

"Well, then," said the superintendent, "I shall come again tomorrow; and if Fanny Crosby does not know them at that time, I shall put her on the mantle." I took his jest in earnest; and the next day all of the tables were learned. Then we went on as far as long division and there my patience failed. I simply could not learn arithmetic, although I tried my best; finally, in utter despair, I said to my teacher,

"I suppose you regard me as a very inattentive pupil." To my surprise, she replied,

"No, I do not, for you can never learn mathematics. Let us go to the superintendent and tell him so!" He was glad to excuse me from other requirements, and it was arranged that I should take an extra study. From that hour I was a new creature: what a nightmare I was escaping! I thoroughly appreciated a parody in one of our arithmetics, which runs as follows:

Multiplication is vexation,
  Division is as bad;
The rule of three puzzles me,
  And fractions make me mad.

As a pleasant contrast I delight to recall our singing classes. A few months after my arrival at the Institution Mr. Anthony Reiff became our teacher; and he remained there for more than forty years as a faithful, efficient and earnest instructor. We loved him dearly, and to him many of his former pupils looked back and called him the master of their youth.

One beautiful, crisp November morning in 1837 we laid the cornerstone of the new Institution building. The mayor, common council, and many prominent citizens came to attend the exercises, as they always did on special occasions. Mr. Reiff composed

a march to some words I had written, part of which
I now recall—

>   This day may every bosom feel
>   A thrill of pleasure and delight;
>   Its scenes will in our memories dwell,
>   When time shall wing his rapid flight.
>
>   May the great being who surveys
>   The countless acts by mortals done,
>   Behold with an approving eye
>   The structure which is now begun.

Before 1840 my friends had nearly spoiled me
with their praises. At least I began to feel my own
importance as a poet a little too much; and so the
superintendent, Mr. Jones, thought something ought
to be done to curb such rising vanity. One morning
after breakfast I was summoned to the office; and,
thinking he would ask me for a poem, or perhaps
give me a word of commendation, as he sometimes
did, I obeyed at once—but instead of more praise
and a new commission to write verses I found a
plain talk awaiting me.

It was an impressive occasion, and I remember
what Mr. Jones said almost word for word:

"Fanny, I am sorry you have allowed yourself to be
carried away by what others have said about your
verses. True, you have written a number of poems
of real merit; but how far do they fall short of the
standard that you might attain. Shun a flatterer,

Fanny, as you would a viper; for no true friend would deceive you with words of flattery. Remember that whatever talent you possess belongs wholly to God; and that you ought to give Him the credit for all that you do."

Mr. Jones was a fine teacher of the young; and he knew just what was best in my particular case. After giving me a little more advice, he said,

"Now, we will reconstruct the fabric—but on a different plan. You have real poetic talent; yet it is crude and undeveloped; and if your talent ever amounts to much, you must polish and smooth your verses so that they may be of more value. Store your mind with useful knowledge; and the time may come, sooner or later, when you will yet attain the goal toward which you have already made some progress."

Then the dear man said to me, "Fanny, have I wounded your feelings?" Something within me bore witness that Mr. Jones spoke the truth; and so I answered,

"No, sir. On the contrary, you have talked to me like a father, and I thank you very much for it."

In years afterward I gradually came to realize that his advice was worth more than the price of rubies; and if I am justified in drawing any analogy from my own experience, I would say that a little kindly advice is better than a great deal of scolding. For a single word, if spoken in a friendly spirit, may be sufficient to turn one from a dangerous error. In the same way, a single syllable, if spoken from a hard heart, may be just enough to drive another from the

true path. This principle has been the foundation of
my work among the missions of New York. I find
that the confidence of the sinner is all that one
needs for the beginning of the work of grace. A man
can be won if he knows that somebody trusts him;
and I firmly believe that faith and love go hand in
hand through the dark places of this world, seeking
the lost, and we not infrequently find them where
we least expect them to be.

6

Inspiration for Work

Not many weeks after the interview with Dr. Jones, he called me to the office one day and said, "You are not to write a line of poetry for three months."

This decision came as a bolt of lightning out of a clear sky; and I was overwhelmed with astonishment, but for six weeks he resolutely enforced his command to the very letter, and at the end of this period I fell into a state of listlessness. My teachers soon noticed that my lessons were unlearned, the result of which was a third summons before the superintendent. Dr. Jones said,

"Fanny, what is the trouble with your lessons? The teachers report that you do not recite as well as you did during the last term. Are you ill?" Before he had fairly finished questioning me, my reply was ready because I had been expecting just such an interview, and so I had made up my mind what to say. I replied,

"I find it impossible to keep my mind on my lessons, for poetry occupies my thoughts in spite of all efforts to think of other things. I cannot help it."

"Well," said the superintendent, "write as much as you like, but pay a little more attention to the morning lectures."

They had been trying me. In those days phrenology was in high favor and as a last attempt to find out whether I was a "born poet" or not, the "science" was brought to bear upon my case, when a favorable opportunity came. This was very soon, the occasion being a visit of the celebrated Dr. Combe of Boston for the purpose of examining the craniums of some of our pupils. There was one boy among them who could listen to two stories, sing a song, and solve a hard problem in mathematics at the same time—at least it was said he could do all that. When the doctor come to him, he exclaimed, "Here is a great mathematician; and some day you will hear from him." Daniel Webster was always greatly admired for his brain power, but he said of himself that he could think of only one thing at once. But our pupil was unlike him in this respect, and also in one other—he never did become famous, as the phrenologist predicted he would.

When Dr. Combe came to look at my head he remarked, "And here is a poetess; give her every possible advantage. Read the best books to her, and teach her to appreciate the best poetry." This was certainly welcome news to me, and it must have had some little effect on my teachers; for they now encouraged me in all the ways wherein they had before tried to dishearten me.

Mr. Hamilton Murray, who at that time was a member of the Board of Managers of the Institution, soon took me into his charge; and I became known to my friends as his "little protégée." His knowledge of the classics was broad, his natural talents superior, and his command of the mother tongue excellent. He read to me from the classics by the hour and advised me to commit long passages to memory; and frequently he gave me the lines of favorite poets to imitate. Most of these, of course, were means to an end; and consequently were soon forgotten. I can, in fact, recall but one, a scrap of verse in the style of Nathaniel P. Willis, whom I was told to imitate in such a way that "it cannot be told from his original poem." The specimen from Willis is called "Morning," and runs as follows,

O could we wake from sorrow,
Were it all a changeful dream like this:
To cast aside like an untimely garment of the morn;
Could the long fever of the soul be cooled
By a sweet breath from nature,
How lightly were the spirit reconciled.

My parody is:

O could we with the gloomy shades of night
Chase the dark clouds of sorrow from the brow;

Could pure affection feel no withering blight,
But heart to heart in one sweet tie be linked,
How were the soul content to fold her wings,
And dwell forever in such loveliness.

The political campaigns in the years between
1840 and 1850 called forth a great amount of versi-
fying. In the autumn of the first-named year General Harrison was elected to the presidency. Every-
body loved the hero of Tippecanoe; and the opposing
party hunted high and low, but they could find not
one thing in his record that might be used against
him. He was the candidate of the Whig party; and I
was an ardent Democrat. One of the interesting
ditties used during the campaign is now remembered by many,

Did you ever hear of a farmer,
Whose cabin's in the West,
Of all the men for President
The wisest and the best?
To put him in the Capitol
We've found a capital way;
O we'll sing our Harrison song by night,
And beat his foes by day.

In my zeal for the Democratic party, I felt it proper
to change the last line into, "And scratch his eyes
by day."

Perhaps the best-remembered song is "Tippecanoe and Tyler, too," the first lines of which are,

> Oh, what has caused this great commotion,
>   motion, motion,
> Our country through?
> It is the ball that's rolling on
> For Tippecanoe and Tyler, too.

But the hero of Tippecanoe lived but a single month to serve his country as president. Evidently the new surroundings at Washington did not agree with him; and he passed away on April 4, 1841. In memory of the sad event I wrote some eulogistic stanzas, which have already been mentioned, in connection with my grandfather's eight-mile walk. As this poem was the best that I had written previous to 1841, I quote it in part:

> He is gone: in death's cold arms he sleeps.
> Our President, our hero brave,
> While fair Columbia o'er him weeps,
> And chants a requiem at his grave;
> Her sanguine hopes are blighted now,
> And weeds of sorrow veil her brow.
>
> Ah, Indiana, where is he,
> Who once thy sons to battle led?
> The red man quailed beneath his eye,
> And from his camp disheartened fled.
> With steady hand he bent the bow
> And laid the warlike savage low.

The forest with his praises rung,
His fame was echoed far and wide—
With loud hurrah his name was sung,
Columbia's hero and her pride.
The tuneful harp is now unstrung
And on the drooping willow hung.

One afternoon at the commencement of our summer vacation our superintendent came in and said that President Tyler, who succeeded General Harrison, was in the reception room; and that the Mayor and Common Council were with him. Well did I know what that meant; and said, "Now, give me ten or fifteen minutes and I shall have the best welcome that I can prepare in so short a time." I recited my poem; then sang a piece; and concluded by reading a song, which I had composed for the previous Fourth of July, all of which I remember is two lines of the chorus,

And this the glad song of our nation shall be,
Hurrah for John Tyler and liberty's tree.

As memory rolls back the curtain of the years I behold again the Institution with its spacious halls that ring with mirth and song, its school rooms filled with happy hearts and smiling faces; the chapel where at morn and eve and on Sabbath days we gathered for religious worship; and the beautiful

playgrounds, from which the clear sound of the bell
called us from our fun to our duty—but a shade of
sadness steals over me, and I ask,

> Where are the friends of my youth,
> Oh, where are those treasured ones gone?

Instantly the names of Cynthia Bullock, Catherine
Kennedy, Mary Mattox, Anna Smith, Imogene Hart,
and Alice Holmes are on my lips. They were among
my earlier associates and their voices come back
mingled with sweet memories of the sunny past:
the murmur of the afternoon breeze; the echo of
the woodland; and the quietness of the twilight.
And now I fancy that we are hastening from the
school room for a fifteen-minute recess; again we
stand together in a group in some remote corner,
repeating the lessons we have learned, and striving
not to forget any of them before tomorrow morning's class, when they will be reviewed. Thus does
the past indeed blend with the present. Life in
those years had few changes for us, and we trusted
the many hopes for the future to a wiser guidance
than our own. Of all this happy company of girls
who were at the New York Institution before 1840,
only Imogene Hart and Alice Holmes and I are
living. Miss Hart possessed a deep love for music,
inherited from her father, under whose judicious
training she was able to sing from many classical
authors before she was ten years old, and I am glad

to know that her voice still retains its sweetness. Judging from the music and poems she sends me from time to time I am confident that she has not lost her old fondness for the "divine arts."

Alice Holmes was a deep thinker, and her genius for mathematics carried her far beyond most of her companions. She was also gifted with a poetic fancy, and has written two beautiful little volumes of poetry since she was with us at the Institution.

I well remember the day she came to us from her home in Jersey City. We were apprised of her coming and determined to give her as good a reception as we could, lest she should become homesick as many of us had been. She was to occupy a portion of my room, and it devolved upon me to make her feel at home; and very soon we were conversing about all sorts of things. I found that she was a member of the Episcopal Church, while I was an adherent of the Methodist; and the contrast between us in this respect suggested a bit of doggerel. Walking demurely toward her couch in the farther end of the room, just as she was about to retire, I said, "Alice, I have a piece of poetry, which I would like you to hear; and will you please tell me how it sounds?" Then I repeated my lines:

> Oh, how it grieves my poor old bones,
> To sleep so near that Alice Holmes,
> I will inform good Mr. Jones,
> I can't sleep with a churchman.

In the course of five or six years our school increased rapidly. When I entered in 1835, I was the thirty-first pupil; before the end of ten years the number was more than one hundred; and in the old building we were packed away in close quarters, but were happy as the birds of a May morning. The new school edifice was completed early in 1841.

Thanksgiving Day was always one of peculiar interest to us, for besides a hearty dinner and reunion of the pupils in the morning, in the evening there was an entertainment to which the Board of Managers were also invited. At one of these social gatherings seven of us girls recited a dialogue that I had written for the occasion. The subject was "New England and New York," and it was dedicated to Mr. James F. Chamberlain, our superintendent, who was a native of Rhode Island. Part of the last chorus, as it was sung to the tune of "Auld Lang Syne," follows:

Should ancient customs be forgot,
And never brought to mind?
In what our fathers loved so well
Can we no pleasure find?
They weave a charm around the heart,
That cannot pass away,
Thanksgiving Day, we love its name,
The dear Thanksgiving Day.

A social band are gathering now
Around the blazing hearth,
And gaily rings their merry laugh

And songs of artless mirth.
Bright moments of unsullied joy,
Oh, could ye longer stay!
Thanksgiving Day, we love its name,
The dear Thanksgiving Day.

The Institution for the Blind, New York

7

The Daily Task

New York City has grown wonderfully in many ways since 1835, and the advance in knowledge and education has been no less rapid than its material prosperity. I well remember the time when Kipp and Brown's stages were the sole means of rapid transit in the city; and they only went up as far as Twenty-sixth Street unless by special order. Our buildings were situated on Thirty-fourth Street and Ninth Avenue in the midst of a delightful suburban district in plain view of the Hudson River and the lawns and fields which gently sloped towards the river.

The rising hour at the Institution was half-past five o'clock during the summer when I first went there; but about 1837 it was changed to six, and some of us found even that hour too early to suit our inclinations. But unless we were able to give a sufficient excuse for being late at morning prayers we were denied our breakfast as a penalty for our tardiness. After breakfast at seven o'clock we enjoyed a lecture on mental and moral philosophy, and the rest of the morning and afternoon was taken up with recitations and singing classes until half-past four. The evening was passed in listening to selections from standard authors.

Sometimes during the breakfast hour they read to us from the newspapers, or we talked over the daring exploit of one of our own number, such as the killing of a mouse by a timid girl; in fact, if any one of us did an act out of the ordinary we heard of it at the breakfast table, and I must confess that I was concerned in many of the practical jokes.

We had a book in the Institution, generally called "a shoe book," but I called it after the name of our shoemaker, "Simpson on the Understanding." In the evening various books were read to us by students from a theological seminary in the city; and after they had finished "Stevens' Travels in the Holy Land" one morning a girl came to me and asked what I thought would be read next. I replied, "Very likely they will read 'Simpson on the Understanding,' which is a fine book; but you had better go and ask the superintendent." This she did, and with a merry laugh he showed her the shoe-book, adding, "That is some of Fanny's work, I know."

We had a postman whom I used to tease in every possible manner. I had never spoken with him in my life; but I would hide the pen and ink and his letter book, which annoyed him so much that he was anxious to see what sort of a being could be so mischievous. Once, while it was raining tremendously,

I wrote the following lines, and placed them where he would be sure to find them:

> Postman, come not yet,
>   Wait till the storm is past,
> Or you'll a ducking get;
>   The rain is falling fast.
>
> You have a new white hat,
>   As I have heard them say;
> Then, postman, think of that!
>   Don't venture out today!
>
> Presumptuous man, in vain
>   To stay your course I sing;
> In spite of wind or rain
>   The letters you will bring;
> Though you are such a dunce
>   I will not cruel be,
> But ask our nurse at once
>   To make some flax-seed tea.

To even scores with me, they sometimes returned a joke at my expense. For example, the superintendent one evening, when I returned home late from a lecture, informed me that there was a "Bridgeport Farmer" in the house, who had come to visit me. Thinking one of my friends had actually arrived during my absence, I went to bed, joyful with the expectation of seeing him early the following morning. To this end I arranged my toilet with unusual care; I went to the office to inquire after my guest; and to my vexation the superintendent handed me a copy of the "Farmer," a newspaper published in Bridgeport, exclaiming, "Here he is; bid him good-morning."

Once when I had infringed upon a rule the super-intendent called me to him, and said that I must retire to my room. I went up stairs singing,

> My glad soul mounted higher
> In a chariot of fire;
> And the moon was under my feet.

He at once called me back, saying, "You are too willing. Don't break any more rules!"

Nor did my daring stop short of the Governor of New York, William H. Seward, who came to inspect our buildings. I thought it would be a capital idea to get him to pick up my ball of yarn, for I happened to be knitting when he called; and so when he was just a little way from me, I managed to drop the ball on the floor. The gracious man picked it up and gave it to me with a good word of encouragement. But one of the teachers saw what I had done and laughingly told Mr. Chamberlain, who remarked, "Oh, don't say anything about it to Fanny, for we never know what she will do next." Yet I must have been more prompt at playing jokes than at learning my lessons, for Mr. Hamilton Murray very often waited several days before I would give him the piece of verse I had promised him. Once when his patience was exhausted by a long delay, he came to me and said,

"Fanny, I am coming up in the morning. Will you have that blank verse ready?"

"Yes, sir," I answered, but it was not ready when he came for it.

"Well," said Mr. Murray, "now we will come to business, no blank verse, no dinner." His threat had the desired effect; the verse was ready in less than an hour.

Thus these trivial incidents helped to make up the joy of life; and I think the poet Keble was certainly right, when he wrote,

> The trivial round, the common task,
> Will furnish all we ought to ask,
> Room to deny ourselves, a road
> To bring us daily nearer God.

We had many important days when famous visitors honored us by coming to see our work. One of the first of these that I remember was Count Henri Gratien Bertrand, the faithful field marshal of the great Napoleon, and his constant companion during his exile at Saint Helena. After the death of his general, Marshal Bertrand accompanied his remains to France, where he was forgiven by the party which had come into power.

A part of the poem which I recited in honor of Marshal Bertrand contained a reference to the death of Napoleon at Saint Helena,

When by those he loved deserted,
   Thine was still a faithful heart;
Thou wert proud to share the exile
   Of the hapless Bonaparte.

Like an angel, whispering comfort,
   Still in sickness thou wert nigh;
And when life's last scenes were over,
   Tears of anguish dimmed thine eye.

"Oh," he exclaimed, "how did you know that I sat with my head in my hands and wept as the life of the great general slowly ebbed away?"

"I did not know it," I replied, "but described the circumstance from imagination." Then he gave me a box containing a piece of the willow that grew above Napoleon's grave. "God bless you," he said in a husky voice, "how I wish you could have known the Emperor!"

I always admired the courage of Napoleon, though I could not love him as a man; and so the devotion of his faithful marshal touched my heart. Personally the visit of Ole Bull was more pleasing to me, for I love music better than the red deeds of war. For an hour the noted Norwegian violinist played from the great masters, and held everyone of us spellbound while he rendered with marvelous sympathy and power all of the selections he loved so dearly.

The general instruction of the blind was a new idea to most persons previous to 1850, and, on this account, we had many curious visitors, but we were always glad to show everyone who came what we could do. As it was one of my duties to conduct them through the buildings, a good many peculiar questions were asked me. Once a lady said,

"There is one place I would like so much to see."

"What is that?" I asked, for we had been the round of all that I thought of interest to strangers.

"Why I am very anxious to see your children eat; how do they find the way to their mouths?"

"O well," I replied quickly, "if that is all, you shall see; send out and get me a piece of cake and I will show you." The same question was put to one of our boys; and he answered it as follows:

"We take a string, tie one end of it to the table leg; the other to our tongue; and then we take the food in our left hand, and feel up the string with our right until we come to our mouth."

Mr. Anthony Reiff, our music teacher, could see perfectly; but, on a certain occasion, while a party of us from the Institution were staying at a hotel, the clerk of the place asked how long he had been "that way." For a joke, the teacher answered, "All my life"; and the mistaken clerk carefully led him up to his room.

But we were also favored with scores of delightful visitors whom we loved to recall in later years. One afternoon the superintendent said to me, "There is a gentleman waiting below, and will you be so kind as to show him through the Institution?" I was only too glad to do so; and we went the rounds of the buildings, until finally the stranger picked up a copy of my book, "The Blind Girl and Other Poems." Not knowing me, he said,

"Oh, here is Miss Crosby's book. You know her

well, I suppose." I admitted that I was acquainted with such a person and decided to have a little sport.

"And is she not very amiable?" was the next question.

"Oh, no; far from it," was my reply.

"Well, I am very sorry to hear that," he said, "but I will take one of her books; and will you please tell her?"

When he was leaving, he handed me his card, and I learned to my utter astonishment that the visitor was the celebrated Professor Tellcamp of Columbia College. The incident immediately brought to mind the scriptural advice, "Be not forgetful to entertain strangers, for thereby some have entertained angels unawares."

I never saw Professor Tellcamp again, and I suppose he did not learn of the joke that I played on him. Not long after his visit I entertained a young student of Columbia College under similar circumstances. The superintendent came up to the room, where several of us were enjoying a delightful book, in no mood to be disturbed; and when he called for volunteers to conduct a stranger through the building there was a silence. Finally I said carefully, "I will take him through, if I like him." When we were introduced I did indeed like him; and we conversed for more than three hours unconscious of the flight of time. He had bright hopes for future usefulness, and I also had my own dreams, so we compared notes together. We did not meet again until sixty years afterward, but both of us were able to recall the minute details of our conversation on that day. He was Dr. Israel Parsons and became a successful physician in one of the beautiful towns of central New York. After our second meeting, we saw each other yearly for several summers at Assembly Park, until the white-robed angel summoned him to the Celestial City.

8

Summer Vacations

In the summer of 1842 it was decided that about twenty of our pupils, accompanied by a few of the Board of Managers, should make a tour into the central part of the state, with the purpose of showing the public to what extent the blind could be educated; and also to induce parents to send their children to our school. This journey took us by way of the "raging canal"; and travel by water before 1850 was very popular. The Erie suited our purpose very well; for we could charter a boat, and tie it up at any town along the way until we were ready to proceed on the following morning, after the exhibition the night before in the town hall. So we had a veritable moving "hotel" at our service.

A few slight inconveniences in our accommodations did not in the least dishearten us, as the novelty of the trip by water made up for whatever household articles were lacking. We had one wash

basin for twenty-three faces; and there was much
rivalry in the morning to see who would be the first
to get *the* basin. In the beginning of our journey the
captain of our boat did not appreciate some of our
practical jokes; before many days had passed, however, we became better acquainted, and then he
could not do enough for our comfort.

Whenever we stopped at a town scores of curious
visitors came to visit us at our "hotel"; consequently by evening the news of our arrival had been
so noised abroad that the town hall was usually
well filled for our evening exhibition. The program
usually included an address of welcome to us,
delivered by some clergyman or other representa-
tive citizen. At Little Falls the duty of introducing
us fell to a lawyer, who referred eloquently to our
visit and to the grand act of the legislature of the
state in "instituting such a wonderful Institution"
as ours in New York City. This became a favorite
phrase at our floating hotel.

My beloved teacher, Mr. Hamilton Murray, used
to introduce me in a beautiful manner; but, when
he was absent, his namesake, Mr. Robert I. Murray,
always, without one single variation, used the following form—"This young woman will now repeat
a piece of her own composition. It has never been
revised or corrected by any of the managers we
know of." There was a perceptible titter among the
audience whenever this form of introduction was
used, but Mr. Murray thought it very strange that I
did not like this method.

"Thee wants Hamilton Murray to introduce thee,"
he would often say, and I always replied,

"Yes, Mr. Murray, I *do*."

The pupils' part of the program consisted in reading from the raised letters, geography, history, arithmetic and singing, and last of all came my poetical address. Skeptical members of the audience often sent involved sentences to the platform to be parsed. At Schenectady someone sent up the following passage from Pope's "Universal Prayer":

> What conscience dictates to be done,
> Or warns me not to do,
> This, teach me more than hell to shun,
> That, more than heaven pursue.

There was a flurry behind the scenes. Some of the managers said that I ought not to try to parse it; but Mr. Murray urged me on; and so I went out upon the platform. The sentence was read: I had never heard it before and for a few moments was completely confused. I suppose the managers thought "I told you so." I began by saying "'what' is an interjection," but I realized at once that I had made a mistake, and, forgetting that there was a single person present besides Mr. Murray, I cried, "No, it isn't any such thing; wait a minute and I will tell you what it is." The audience laughed and, of course, added to my confusion, but, after thinking a few minutes, I transposed the sentence correctly, and then was able to parse it without any trouble. When the program was finished, a gentleman came up to me, spoke kindly of my success in being able to unravel the knotty syntax of Pope's lines, and then placed a five-dollar gold piece in my hand. Before I could inquire his name he had vanished, but I always thought that he was a teacher in Union College.

A restless mortal like myself had to be doing something continually while we were away on these long journeys. One morning we stopped at a town near which the grandmother of one of our pupils lived; so he and I thought it would be a capital idea to make the matron of our children believe that the old lady had come to visit him. Mr. Murray had taught me to disguise my voice so well that the matron was completely deceived. When we knew that she had retired to take her usual afternoon nap, we stationed ourselves where she could overhear what was said. "O Charlie, you had your grand-mother to see you," said the matron when she came out; and we managed to restrain our mirth, until later in the day we could keep the secret no longer.

While we were passing through the lovely val-ley in which the Mohawk River flows, one of the teachers asked me to sing Tom Moore's "Meeting of the Waters"; and Mr. Chamberlain described the beautiful scenery that lay on every hand,

and I changed the first line of the Irish bard's poem

> Sweet vale of Avoka,

into

> Sweet vale of the Mohawk,

and then continued the quotation,

> How calm could I rest
> In thy bosom of shade with the friend I love best,
> Where the storms which we feel in this cold world
>   shall cease,
> And our hearts, like thy waters, be mingled in
>   peace.

At last we arrived at Niagara where nature has composed her mightiest poem. The grandeur of the surroundings inspired within my heart a reverence such as nothing else in the world has ever awakened; and when we again visited the enchanted spot in the following summer my joy was increased. I could picture it all in my imagination. Across the gorge were the woods and fields of the Canadian shore; almost at our feet was that tremendous mass of water plunging directly downward and dashing itself on the rocks one hundred and sixty feet below; and above the falls hung a delicate mist in the sunlight that reflected the countless colors of both earth and sky. While I stood there, completely lost amid the marvelous works of God, Mr. Murray

requested me to repeat a poem that had been composed during the previous summer; and while I said
over my humble lines we lifted our hearts in
thankfulness to the kind Father of us all,

> Who spread'st the azure vault above,
> Whose hand controls the boistcrous sea.

At evening we went down to Lewiston and from
there crossed to the Canadian shore to visit the
beautiful city of Toronto. Once again during this
trip, as during the return journey from New York, I
saw some of the colors of the golden sunlight glowing on the waters.

After the summer vacation of 1843 my health
began to decline to such an extent that my teachers
became alarmed. They were not aware that most of
the nights in the previous spring did not find me in
bed until twelve, sometimes two o'clock; and when
we returned from the trip through central New York
I renewed my midnight vigils with the inevitable
result: my strength gradually failed. It was not many
weeks, however, before the cause of my trouble
became known to Dr. Clements. At first he said
that I must not work out of school hours; then he
refused to allow me to hear any classes; and finally
decided to send me into the country to rest awhile
during the summer of 1844.

Meanwhile I had been working on my book, and

it was issued just before the final mandate not to do any work at all. As a preliminary to publishing a volume of poems, they told me I must have my daguerreotype taken for the frontispiece. In those days no less than four minutes were required for an exposure; and the idea that I, the restless Fanny Crosby, as they all knew me, would be obliged to sit still so long—well that was indeed very funny. As a result I burst into a laugh right in the midst of my "sitting"; and, of course, spoiled a plate for the photographer. Then the tedious process began again; a veritable inquisition it was for me, but finally I endured to the length of five whole minutes and secured a fine picture.

It was with great reluctance that I consented to have my poems published; for I realized only too well that they were unfinished productions; and I hoped to improve upon them in time. But a few of the teachers and managers at the Institution would not take no for an answer; and, consequently, the work went forward. Mr. Hamilton Murray wrote the introduction and Dr. J. W. G. Clements did the compiling, which was all the more kind of him since he had a large practice and could spare but a moment now and then to listen to my dictation.

Many of the verses in "The Blind Girl and Other Poems" were autobiographic, such, for instance, as the opening lines of the book:

Her home was near an ancient wood,
Where many an oak gigantic stood;

And fragrant flowers of every hue
In that sequestered valley grew.

A church there reared its little spire,
And in their neat and plain attire,
The humble farmers would repair
On Sabbath morn to worship there.

My schoolmates were also pictured:

With their laugh the woodland rang,
Or if some rustic air they sang,
These rural notes of music sweet
The woodland echoes would repeat.

But the labor in publishing a book was too great
for my strength; and when I went into the country
in the summer of 1844, many of my companions
thought that they were certainly bidding me good-
bye for the last time. Dr. Clements also feared that
my health would not improve; he said that I needed
rest and petting more than medicine; and when I
was ready to start for home he said,

"Can you get plenty of pure milk at your mother's home?" I assured him that I could; and he
added,

"Well, drink as much as you can." His good
advice was followed and at the beginning of the
next term I returned to the Institution in perfect
health.

Four years after I first went to New York a little

sister came to gladden our home, but the angel of
death soon called her away to that other home
above. The letter that I wrote to my mother and my
step-father enclosing a poem, is still preserved as it
was originally copied by Mr. Chamberlain. Concerning the death of my little sister, I said: "The
impression that her death has made upon my mind
is a deep one; but this event teaches me a lesson,
which, I trust, I never shall forget. Once I looked
forward to future years, when she would be not only
a comfort to you but also to myself; but these fond
hopes are blighted. Let us not repine, but cheerfully
submit to the will of Heaven."

The poem that I sent to mother is as follows:

She's gone, ah yes, her lovely form
　　Too soon has ceased to bloom,
An emblem of the fragile flower
　　That blossoms for the tomb.

Yet, mother, check that starting tear,
　　That trembles in thine eye;
And thou, kind father, cease to mourn,
　　Suppress that heaving sigh.

She's gone, and thou, dear aunt, no more
　　Wilt watch her cradle bed,
She slumbers in the peaceful tomb,
　　But weep not for the dead.

Kind uncle, thou art grieving too,
　　Thy tears in thought I see;
Ah, never will her infant hand
　　Be stretched again to thee.

Mrs. Crosby, Fanny and her two younger sisters

She's gone, yet why should we repine,
  Our darling is at rest;
Her cherub spirit now reclines
  On her Redeemer's breast.

Sometimes two or three of my associates would accompany me when I went home for the summer vacation; and mother liked them to come as often as possible for she loved the society of young people. A humorous incident happened during one of these visits that is good enough to relate here. Among my friends came a young man who wore a wig, but mother did not know it; and one evening, when there were several present, he complained of a severe cold in his head.

"O I think I can cure that," said my mother. He replied,

"Never mind; I'll get over it." But she was evidently bent upon working a cure; and despite the remonstrance of the young man, proceeded to rub some salt on his scalp, whereupon the fact of the wig became known to the company. The young man was considerably embarrassed; and mother of course heartily wished she had let him alone.

My two little sisters were always in ecstasy whenever I came home. They saved up their pennies for weeks that they might buy me some sweetmeats. And such chattering: there was so much important news to be told and so many questions, on both sides, that required immediate answers. Too soon would come the end of these summer outings; and my heart always trembled when the hour of parting arrived; for I could hear in the distance, as the carriage bore me away, the plaintive voices crying "Fanny, Fanny, come back!" More than once the old homesickness returned; and I was again sorely tempted to turn back from the journey to New York.

But it is a rare blessing that these dear sisters have been spared, so that the reality of the present is no less gracious than the memory of the past. The days of childhood are recalled as a benediction; and the daily ministry of the present is a true manifestation of the love between those who are near and dear to me.

While our precious mother lived, her birthdays were occasions of festive gatherings; and almost yearly I wrote her a poem. That which was written for her eighty-second birthday follows:

How pleasant to look on a brow like hers,
    With hardly a trace of care;
How cheerful the light of her beaming eye,
    As she sits in her easy chair.

So little the change in her dear, kind face
    We scarce can believe it true
That she numbers today her four score years,
    Her four score years and two.

Her winter of age, though the snowflakes fell,
    Has never been dark and drear,
She moves with the vigor of younger feet,
    And her mind is bright and clear.

She merrily talks of the olden time,
  Of the friends in youth she knew;
She is sprightly and gay, though she numbers today
  Her four score years and two.

And now as we come with our birthday gifts,
  When she views them o'er and o'er,
And the earnest God bless you, my children dear,
  Is breathed from her lips once more.

We think how devoted our mother's love,
  What a sunshine of joy she gives,
And we feel as we tenderly kiss her cheek,
  What a comfort that still she lives!

9

Two Addresses Before Congress

But I have passed over two or three important events. During the autumn of 1843, as I have said, I was ill; and when a party from the school was going to Washington to appear before Congress, in the following January, I had not yet fully recovered. Dr. Clements said that I would fret myself into a serious sickness if they left me at home; besides the trip South might do me some good. It was finally decided by the Board of Managers that he should go and take charge of me, to which arrangement I joyfully assented; yet, when I learned that I was expected to deliver a poem before a joint session of both houses of Congress, my heart sank within me. Indeed I think I would not have agreed to the arrangement, were it not for the fact that our party were trying to impress upon the legislators in Washington the absolute need of schools for the blind in every state of the Union. Any chance of doing a little for them I, of course, would not let pass; and

so there I was a timid mortal not in the best of
health, to deliver an address before the most distinguished body I have ever seen. Some of the skeptical
managers said that I would fail in the midst of my
recitation, and that thought, I must confess, was in
my own mind. But the inspiration of the hour was
sufficient to fortify me against the dreaded failure.
At any rate I tried to do my level best; and when I
finished my poem there was a dreadful silence which
I interpreted to mean that the audience was not
pleased. With mingled emotions, alternating between hope and fear, I waited, it seemed to me, as
long as five minutes; in reality I suppose, not more
than thirty seconds passed before there was such a
tremendous applause that I was actually frightened.
At length they began to call for me, and then there
was a hasty consultation in the anteroom between
Dr. Clements and the managers.

"Don't let her try it," they said; "tell them that
she is not strong enough."

But the good doctor asked that the whole matter
be referred to me.

"Yes," I answered, "I will recite another poem, for
never may I get a chance to address such a famous
audience again."

Then, I went out upon the platform, and repeated
some lines that had been written and published the
summer before in memory of the Hon. Hugh S.
Legaré, the lamented Secretary of State, who died
quite suddenly while going, with President Tyler, to
attend the exercises at the laying of the cornerstone

of the Bunker Hill monument. I will quote three
stanzas of my tribute:

> Farewell, esteemed departed one, farewell,
> Deep solemn tones have pealed thy funeral knell—
> Thou to the grave art gone. Sweet be thy rest!
> For angels guard the relics of the blest.
>
> Hark, hark, thy requiem floats upon the ear,
> So deeply sad. We pause; we weep to hear.
> Ye patriot sons of fair Columbia's shore,
> A brilliant star has set, to shine no more.
>
> Weep, oh, Columbia, o'er his lonely grave,
> Then let the cypress, sorrow's emblem, wave,
> The mournful breezes sigh, wild flowerets bloom,
> And breathe their fragrance o'er his hallowed tomb.

My lines of tribute evidently took the senators by
surprise, and I was told that many of them wept.
But the occasion was doubly sad for me, because
the sister of Secretary Legaré was in the audience,
having come all the way from Georgia to see our
pupils, and to meet the writer of the poem, for she
had already seen it in the papers. When I came out
of the Senate chamber she met me at the door and
placed a beautiful ring on my finger. The following
year she came to New York to visit us and I had the
pleasure of presenting her with the first copy of
"The Blind Girl and Other Poems" that came from
the press. In April, 1847, we again appeared before
Congress, with delegations from Boston and Phila-

delphia institutions, and Laura Bridgman was a member of the party. I shall never forget her gentle manners and her faculty of remembering people. On the night of our Washington concert she shook hands with six congressmen, whose names were written on her palm. In a few minutes they again passed before her, though in different order, and she was able to tell the name of each without any difficulty.

During our stay in Washington we had the privilege of hearing the last speech of John Quincy Adams. The audience was so still that the faintest noise in any part of the room seemed to be very loud, and we waited breathlessly to hear what the aged statesman would say to the rising generation. His voice had lost much of its original sweetness and power but it fell on our ears with a strange cadence that echoed in my memory for many years after the voice itself had ceased to be a great and commanding force in the councils of our nation.

James K. Polk was then president; and the members of our party felt somewhat acquainted with him inasmuch as he had made us a visit during the summer of 1845. On that former occasion I welcomed him with a poem, only the first two lines of which I now remember:

We welcome not a monarch with a crown upon his
    brow,
Before no haughty tyrant as suppliants we bow.

A friend has recently sent me another little impromptu poem which I composed on being given a poke-weed by a friend:

> A thousand thanks to thee, good Mr. Chase,
> This poke-weed garland on my brow I'll place.
> If I this moment Mr. Polk could see
> Quickly an office I'd obtain for thee.
> Once more a thousand thanks from me,
> But, Mr. Chase, a Whig thou must not be.
> Then, change at once thy politics, I pray,
> And I'll send word to Polk without delay.

While we were in Washington, in 1847, President Polk invited us to the White House, and during the course of the conversation, he said,

"Well, Miss Crosby, have you made any poetry since I saw you last year?"

"Yes sir," I promptly replied, "I have composed a song and dedicated it to you."

My announcement was as much of a surprise to my friends as to Mr. Polk himself; for I had kept my own counsel; but he appeared to be much gratified and asked me to take his arm and proceed to the music room, where we held an impromptu recital.

During this appearance before Congress they requested me to recite a poem; and I gladly consented. Some of my friends have maintained that I am the only woman who has appeared before the joint session of the Senate and House of Representatives to present a petition.

On our return trip from Washington, Mr. J. F. Chamberlain, already mentioned as the genial super-

intendent of our Institution, and I happened to
be conversing about the infinite possibilities of
development in the Western part of our country.
"Have you heard my poem, 'Away to the Prairie'?"
asked Mr. Chamberlain. I had not; and he therefore
recited the beautiful stanzas which here follow:

> Away to the prairie, up, up and away,
> Where the bison are roaming, the deer are at play;
> From the wrongs that surround us, the home of our
>   rest,
> Let us seek on the wide, rolling plains of the West.
> Away to the prairie, where the pioneer's lay
> Is echoed afar on the breezes; away!
>
> To the wide, rolling plains of the West let us hie,
> Where the clear river's bosom immirrors the sky,
> On whose banks stands the warrior so brave,
> Whose bark hath alone left a curl on the wave.
>
> Yes, away to the prairie, whose bosom, though wild,
> Is unstained by oppression, by fraud undefiled;
> From the wrongs that surround us, the home of our
>   rest,
> Let us seek on the wide, rolling plains of the West.

I asked him to hum the melody to these words.
Mr. Chamberlain replied that there was no melody
yet composed. "But why can't you write one?" said
he. The suggestion was opportune; for there was
already an air singing itself in my mind; and before
New York was reached the music was completed.

Though our song was popular in the Institution for a number of years it never was made public. In those days I used to play the guitar, the piano and sometimes for our choruses the chapel organ. Special occasions required some original words and music, some of which were a New Year serenade for Mr. Chamberlain; a Thanksgiving chorus; a farewell song to Mr. George F. Root, on his departure for Europe; a quartet, entitled, "Dream of Tomorrow"; a hymn for an infant class, words and music, for Mr. Bradbury in 1867, "Jesus, Dear, I Come to Thee"; a "Welcome to Springtime," 1901, and others.

10

A Peerless Trio of Public Men

For the country at large and for our Institution in particular the year 1848 was an important one. The nation was entering upon a new era of prosperity after the Mexican War; and all eyes were turning towards the South, to face the grim prospect of another dreadful conflict, this time, however, within our own borders, a struggle that was to decide once for all a number of the great questions in dispute. Already there was some talk of disunion— but we all anxiously hoped that our statesmen might yet devise some way out of the difficulty. The discussion of important national affairs was very interesting to our pupils, and many of us were as prolific in compromise measures as was Henry Clay himself; until it seemed that we had arrived at a more satisfactory solution to the problem than any of the great senators at Washington.

At this period, when we were so much interested in public affairs, it was an added source of satisfaction for us to receive visits from a peerless trio of statesmen, all of whom were taking a prominent part in the councils of our nation. One of these men was president of the United States and the other two wanted to be. They were James K. Polk, Henry Clay and Winfield Scott. After serving a number of years in Congress, Mr. Polk had been elected governor of Tennessee; and when a compromise candidate for president had been suggested in 1844, he was nominated against Clay and triumphantly elected.

We regretted very much not being able to see Henry Clay in the Senate, but in the following spring, in March of 1848, he made a tour of the large cities, and as a specially invited guest when in New York came to our Institution. About thirteen months before this time, his beloved son and namesake had fallen while fighting at the battle of Buena Vista; and I had written a poem in memory of Colonel Clay which Mr. Chamberlain sent to his father. The great statesman was never quite himself after his son's death; and I purposely avoided all mention of it in the address of welcome on the day he came to visit us, lest I might wound the heart of the man whom I had learned not only to venerate but to love; for Mr. Clay was always an especial favorite among public men.

There was a strength in his character and an earnestness in his speeches that appealed to me more than I can tell. I used to liken Clay to Richard Henry Lee, and Webster to Patrick Henry; for one was as gentle as the murmur of a rippling stream, the other rushed onward with the strength of a

mountain torrent, sweeping all before him by the
force of his mighty intellect. I thought Clay the
more winning of the two; and I would have chal-
lenged any person, whether Whig or Democrat,
Northerner or Southerner, to come within range of
that man's eloquence without being moved to admiration and profound respect; for his personal mag-
netism was wonderful.

Mr. Clay came to the Institution at about ten
o'clock in the morning, and we were prepared to
welcome him in princely style. When he came in
the door the band greeted him with "Hail to the
Chief"; and, then, they opened their ranks and
allowed him to pass between two files of musicians
to the chapel upstairs where the rest of us were
assembled. We sang a chorus prepared for the occasion, after which Mr. Chamberlain gave some eloquent words of greeting; and, next, came my poem
of welcome.

When I had finished reciting it, Mr. Clay stepped
forward and, drawing my arm in his own, led me
slowly to the front of the platform. "This is not the
only poem," said he, "for which I am indebted to
this lady. Six months ago she sent me some lines on
the death of my dear son." His voice trembled; he
did not speak for some moments, while both of us
stood there weeping. Finally, with a great effort, he
controlled his emotion and delivered one of the
most eloquent addresses to which I have ever listened.
He had a deep rich voice that echoed with strange
sweetness throughout our chapel as it rose and fell

with the feeling that he sought to express, and we were charmed by his eloquence.

Not many months after his visit to New York, Mr. Clay was again elected to the United States Senate, and the old fire seemed to return to him when he arose to debate some important measure, or to propose some great compromise, like the "Omnibus Bill" which bore his own name. Still his health was impaired, and soon afterward he slept with his fathers at Ashland, Kentucky; but the laurels of his fame are blooming yet in all of their original sweetness and beauty.

> Sleep on, oh, statesman, sleep,
> Within thy hallowed tomb,
> Where pearly streamlets glide,
> And summer roses bloom.

In the early spring of 1848 General Scott made a triumphal entry into New York which was almost as notable as that other entry into the city of the Montezumas. The events of the Mexican war were still fresh in our minds, and we were eager to meet the hero who had won the name of "Old-Rough-and-Ready." He came, however, a little before we were prepared for him; still there was no emergency for which our superintendent, Mr. Chamberlain, was not equal. He received the distinguished guest in his usual urbane way, and then sent for me to entertain him until the time set for the afternoon

exercises. From such an honor I shrank at first, but
the great general had not spoken half a dozen sentences before I was at ease; his quiet and kindly
manner was so reassuring.

Mr. Chamberlain's formal address to General Scott
was a model of his excellent use of the English
tongue; and the closing sentences of it have a peculiar force, as I write fifty-six years later and record
the fulfillment of the prophecy therein contained. I
quote from a newspaper of the time:

"Some of these pupils, when you have filled up
the measure of your fame, and to you, the praise
and censure of men will be alike indifferent—they
will survive; and when they shall recount your
achievements, and tell to coming generations of
Chippewa, and of Cerro Gordo, and of Contreras,
and many other fields where you have covered the
proud flag of your country with imperishable glory—I
would have them say, too, that once at least it was
their fortune to listen to the tones of that voice,
whose word of command was ever to the brave the
talisman of assured victory."

General Scott's reply was earnest but brief, and
his gentle manner did not indicate a hero of so
many battles; yet there was strength beneath the
exterior appearance, and a heart of iron within his
breast. But from him I learned that the warrior only
it is, who can fully appreciate the blessing of peace.
I recalled the newspaper reports of the triumphal
entry of the Americans into the city of Mexico, and
how the soldiers reveled there.

"General Scott," I said, "when you found yourself

really within the halls of the Montezumas, did you not feel like shouting?"

"No," replied the soldier, "we felt like falling down here on our knees to thank the good Lord for our victory." Later in the afternoon he said, "No, we did not revel in the halls of Montezumas; we lived on one meal a day."

While General Scott was examining a collection of maps that were used by our pupils, one of the aldermen present—for they always came to our receptions—stepped to my side and whispered,

"The general's sword is just a little out of place."

"Let us remove it quietly," said I. With his aid I carefully drew it out of the great sheath without attracting attention; and then suddenly held it above the head of the intrepid warrior.

"General Scott," I exclaimed in an authoritative tone, "you are my prisoner." Although taken completely by surprise, he was by no means at a loss for an answer.

"Oh, I surrender; I always surrender at discretion to the ladies." He laughed good-naturedly, as did those who saw the incident; and we turned the subject. A moment later, however, he said,

"Well, Miss Crosby, the next time I come here I suppose some young man will have run off with you." Forgetting that he was a candidate for the presidency, I exclaimed,

"Oh, no, I shall wait for the next president." This announcement on my part was followed by a tremendous roar of laughter, and I found myself in an uncomfortable position.

But General Scott, being the candidate of the Whigs at the election of 1852, was defeated by one of his subordinate generals in the Mexican war, Franklin Pierce, of whose political party I was an adherent. Consequently, after the election I wrote a little song entitled, "Carry Me On," most of which has been forgotten, except the chorus, which goes as follows:

> O Whigs, carry me on, carry me far away,
> For election's past and I'm *pierced* at last:
> The *locoes* have gained the day.

I have already mentioned James K. Polk, who was president from 1845 to 1849, and also the soiree at the White House during the Washington exhibition in the winter of 1847. The following summer Mr. Polk returned our call, coming unexpectedly and unattended, for he was a very plain man and did not wish any ceremony at his reception. He said that he had simply come to our beautiful retreat to escape the turmoil of the busy city.

After dinner I asked President Polk if he would not enjoy a stroll through our grounds. Everything that day was in the height of its beauty, the trees formed a double arch over the walks in our yard, and in the lofty boughs many robins and bluebirds built their nests and entertained us with their sweet carols. The soft winds came stealing through the leafy boughs, laden with perfume from the flowers of a score of nearby gardens.

We had not gone many yards before I heard the familiar voice of an old domestic to whom I was indebted for many favors. The dear old woman was not at that time in the employ of the Institution, but had just returned for a few minutes to speak with some of us; and I knew that I might not see her again for months to come. This thought was uppermost in my mind at that moment; and so I turned impulsively to President Polk and said, "Will you please excuse me a minute?" "Certainly," he replied; and so I left the chief man of the nation standing alone while I ran to greet my friend. Realizing my discourtesy on my return, I made all manner of apologies; and tried to explain the circumstance as best I might. To my surprise, however, the great and good man said,

"You have done well, and I commend you for it. Kindness, even to those in the humblest capacity of life, should be our rule of conduct; and by this act you have won not only my respect but also my esteem." I had hitherto held a high opinion of President Polk but from that moment his kind words elevated him to my own ideal of a Christian gentleman; and that night, ere I sought my pillow, I fervently prayed that God would bless and sustain our worthy president in the arduous duty of executing the laws for more than twenty millions of people.

I have already said that I sympathized with the Democratic party. In 1844 Clay and Frelinghuyson were the Whig candidates. One afternoon during the summer I was sitting in the parlor singing snatches of Democratic songs for my own amusement; and, before I knew it, two gentlemen came into the room, one of whom advanced toward me with the request that I favor them with another song. When I had finished singing, he said,

"Then Mr. Clay is not your candidate."

"No," I replied, "but I have a profound respect and reverence for him, and also for Mr. Frelinghuyson— yet they are not my candidates." At that moment Mr. Chamberlain came up and presented me to the two strangers; and to my utter consternation I found that on of them was Mr. Frelinghuyson himself.

"Mr. Frelinghuyson," I said, "you have heard me express my views already; and for me to say that I did not mean it would be telling a falsehood. But I would not have said what I did, had I known you were present—so please take it for what it is worth." He laughed heartily and replied, "I give you credit for your candor."

My interest in public affairs has never abated. There are not many people living in this year of grace who had the privilege of meeting such statesmen as Henry Clay, General Scott, and President Polk; but the names of these heroes are recorded with indelible letters among the annals of our national history and their imperishable deeds are chronicled in characters that no person living should wish to efface. They were men of sterling worth and firm integrity, of whom the rising generation may well learn wisdom and the true principles of national honor and democracy that all of them labored so faithfully to inculcate. And that the men of this present age and of generations to come will continue to remember the dignity and honor that the past has bequeathed to our own and future times, no loyal American need have one iota of doubt.

11

Contrasted Events

Not many months after the visit of General Scott vague rumors of the spread of Asiatic cholera came to our ears. By autumn the dread disease had swept all over Europe slaying its thousands and putting the inhabitants of the infected cities into a panic. The winter of 1848 was favorable to the spread of cholera; a mild, damp, muggy atmosphere prevailed, and the physicians in our city began to predict that we were certain to be visited by the terrible scourge within the year. In 1832 our land had been stricken with cholera and I remembered well the sad reports that reached our little hamlet at Ridgefield from week to week.

For many months, while the black cloud now seemed to be hanging over the defenseless towns of America, we hoped that we might be spared from its ravages, but I think the cholera reached New York in March or April of 1849. At first it was confined to the lower part of the city, where the authorities tried vigorously to stamp it out, meanwhile endeavoring to keep the matter as quiet as possible for fear of unduly alarming the people.

One morning in June Mr. Chamberlain came running into the office; and he was so excited that we thought something dreadful had occurred. I followed him and he said, "Will you promise not to tell what has happened?" I answered in the affirmative; and then he unfolded a pitiful story of a man who had been taken in our very midst; and how they had hurried him to the nearest hospital—a common cart being the only vehicle that could be immediately secured—but the poor sufferer had died on the way. Then we knew that the disease might enter our school at any moment; in which case we feared a terrible mortality among the pupils, for none of them had left for the summer vacation.

On the following Monday we had our first case. One of the youngest girls was taken; she called me to her and asked me to hold her in my lap, as I had been accustomed to do.

"Miss Crosby, I am going home," she said, "and I just wanted to bid you good-bye and to tell you I love you. Now lay me down again." Toward evening she died and before sunrise the next morning we carried her to Trinity Cemetery, where a brief prayer was said; and then, just as the dawn was coming across the eastern hills, our little company slowly wended its way back to the Institution to await the next case.

Dr. J. W. G. Clements was one of the most skillful physicians that the city afforded; but medicine was almost powerless to check the ravages of cholera, except it were used merely as a preventative. I assisted as volunteer nurse, and helped the doctor make some of the remedies. One of them was composed of three parts mercury and one part opium, rolled into pills: I remember that we made six hundred in one day. At the appearance of anything like a symptom of cholera we administered very generous doses of these pills, which proved to be efficient remedies in half of our twenty cases, ten terminating fatally.

I shudder when I recall those days; for frequently the stillness of the night, while I was watching at some bedside, would be broken by the hoarse cry, "Bring out your dead," from some of the city officials as they knocked at the door of a bereaved household. Once, as I was entering the sick room, I struck my foot against an object, which I instantly recognized as a coffin awaiting the morning burial.

When the fourth of July came Dr. Clements and Mr. Chamberlain insisted that I was to go to Brooklyn for a short rest. But at the end of three days I was summoned back to the Institution to welcome, with the customary poem, the great Irish temperance advocate, Father Matthew; and the brief sojourn of the grand old man in our midst was like the visit of an angel to a house of death.

"Daughter, are you from Ireland?" he asked after I had warmly praised the deeds of his countrymen in their struggle for independence.

"No," I was obliged to reply, "but I love Ireland." Then the kind patriarch of temperance laid his hand reverently on my head, and his touch seemed to me like that of a saint who had been permitted to leave his abode in heaven for one single moment to cheer the desolate children of earth.

Not many days after his visit I felt that I had some of the symptoms of cholera myself; and during the day I walked about a great deal and took a large quantity of the cholera pills; for I was well aware that yielding to the disease practically meant death. Yet I did not tell any of those around me, lest I should frighten them; but I excused myself at six o'clock saying that I had been several nights almost without any sleep; and after a good night's rest, at eight the following morning, I awakened to find myself in perfectly normal health. When, however, it became known that I had been in danger of the disease, there was a hasty consultation, after which, Mr. Chamberlain announced that I was to leave for the country on the first of August.

So I left the sorrowing city, which had been almost depopulated by the departure of all who could possibly retire to a safer place, until the frosts of November should kill the epidemic. There were two new cases at the Institution after I left, and three deaths; but about two weeks later the twenty pupils who remained were taken to Whitlockville, New York, for the rest of the summer. In late October the mayor of New York wrote a very beautiful letter asking his scattered people to return to their homes because the danger was past; and so, early in November, our little family were again united.

But I leave these sad events and now turn back almost ten years, to 1839 and the class meetings at the Eighteenth Street Methodist Church. Some of us used to go down there regularly, and on Thursday evening of each week a leader came from that church to conduct a class in the Institution. In those days I was timid and never spoke in public, when I could possibly avoid it; and I must confess that I had grown somewhat indifferent to the means of grace, so much so, in fact, that I attended the meetings and played for them on the condition that they should not call on me to speak.

But one evening the leader brought a young man with him and he was destined to have an important influence on my life. He was Mr. Theodore Camp, a teacher in the city schools; and a man noted for his generous public spirit. From the beginning of our acquaintance I found him a true friend; and I used to consult him concerning all matters in which I was undetermined how to act. In 1845 he was placed in charge of our industrial department; and then we used to attend the class meetings together, but he never urged me in religious matters. And yet I owe my conversion to that same friend, in so far as I owe it to any mortal. By a strange dream I was aroused from a comparative state of indifference. Not that the dream had any particular effect, in itself, except as the means of setting me to thinking. It seemed that the sky had been cloudy for a number of days; and finally someone came to me and said that Mr. Camp desired to see me at once.

Then I thought I entered the room and found him very ill.

"Fanny, can you give up our friendship?" he asked.

"No, I cannot; you have been my advisor and friend and what could I do without your aid?"

"But," replied he, "why would you chain a spirit to earth when it longs to fly away and be at rest?"

"Well," I replied, "I cannot give you up of myself but I will seek divine assistance."

"But will you meet me in heaven?"

"Yes, I will, God helping me," I replied; and I thought his last words were, "Remember you promise a dying man!" Then the clouds seemed to roll from my spirit, and I awoke from the dream with a start. I could not forget those words, "Will you meet me in heaven?" and although my friend was perfectly well I began to consider whether I could really meet him, or any other acquaintance in the better land, if called to do so.

The weeks sped on until the autumn of 1850 when revival meetings were being held in the Thirtieth Street Methodist Church. Some of us went down every evening; and, on two occasions, I sought peace at the altar, but did not find the joy I craved, until one evening, November 20, 1850, it seemed to me that the light must indeed come then or never; and so I arose and went to the altar alone. After a prayer was offered, they began to sing the grand old consecration hymn,

> Alas, and did my Savior bleed,
>
> And did my Sovereign die?

And when they reached the third line of the fourth stanza, "Here Lord, I give myself away," my very soul was flooded with a celestial light. I sprang to my feet, shouting "hallelujah," and then for the first time I realized that I had been trying to hold the world in one hand and the Lord in the other.

But my growth in grace was very slow from the beginning. The next Thursday evening I gave a public testimony at our class meeting; when I finished the tempter said to me, "Well, Fanny, you made a good speech, didn't you?" and I realized at once that this was the old pride returning again to reign in my heart. For a few days I was greatly depressed until a kind friend suggested that I must "go back and do the first works quickly," which meant that I had not made a complete surrender of my will; and then I promised to do my duty whenever the dear Lord should make it plain to me.

But not many weeks later Mr. Stephen Merritt asked me to close one of our class meetings with a brief prayer. My first thought was "I can't"; then the voice of conscience said, "but your promise"; and from that hour, I believe I have never refused to pray or speak in a public service, with the result that I have been richly blessed.

Literary and Musical Memories

Now and then during the early forties I contributed poems to the "Saturday Evening Post" and the "Clinton Signal," for which paper Mr. J. F. Chamberlain and Mr. F. J. Warner also wrote; and the compositor was continually confusing the initials of our names, so that it was sometimes difficult for our friends to tell just which of us wrote a certain piece. Mr. William Wye Smith wrote for the "Saturday Emporium," under the name of "Rusticus," and I answered him, using my own name. He afterwards became a Congregational clergyman and the translator of the Bible into the old Scotch language; and he is still living in St. Catharines, Ontario. I also wrote occasionally for the "Fireman's Journal," a weekly supported by the volunteer companies of New York, in which I took an ardent interest. Most of my poems, in those years, were imaginative and sentimental; and one of them, which I now happen to remember, begins like this,

Let me die on the prairie, and o'er my rude grave
'Mid the soft winds of summer, the tall grass shall
    wave;
I would breathe my last sigh, when the bright hues
    of even
Are fading away in the blue arch of heaven.

During these years we received visits from a large number of literary men and women, among them Thurlow Weed, Mrs. Sigourney and Bayard Taylor.

One bright morning in April, when the violets were opening their tiny buds to the warm sunshine of early spring, the Mayor, Common Council, and a part of the Legislature came to make their annual call. With them also came Martin T. Tupper, the English poet, who at that time was a very popular author of a proverbial philosophy in verse. He was asked to make an address; but, not being adept at extempore speaking, he told us that he would rather recite one of his poems; and he chose one entitled, "Never Give Up," the first stanza of which runs as follows:

Never give up, it is wiser and better
Always to hope than once to despair,
Throw off the yoke with its conquering fetter,
Yield not a moment to sorrow or care,
Never give up, though adversity presses,
Providence wisely has mingled the cup;
And the best counsel in all our distresses
Is the stout watchword, Never give up.

But when Mr. Tupper reached the third line of his poem he broke down; and as I happened to be familiar with it, and was sitting directly behind him, I prompted him. Then he began again, and this time reached the third line of the second stanza, when his memory failed a second time. I repeated the line; but, evidently not wishing to continue, in spite of his title—"Never Give Up"—he turned to the audience and said:

"It is of no use; this lady knows my poem better than I do myself; and therefore I will sit down."

"William Cullen Bryant is coming to our musical" was the watchword that passed through the Institution one day in 1843; and teachers, as well as pupils, could hardly restrain their impatience until the hour of the evening entertainment. We knew Mr. Bryant by reputation, as the able editor of the "Evening Post" for almost twenty years; and we had been delighted by the stories of travel in foreign lands which he occasionally wrote. For about twenty-five years he had been recognized by all classes as the foremost living American poet; and he was frequently called "the first citizen of the Republic." "Thanatopsis" was a household classic, and is said to be the sweetest apology for death that our literature affords. And the very hand of death had been stayed and the gray-haired patriarch spared to enjoy the plaudits of his countrymen. But the mind of a man of the caliber of Bryant is never turned aside, either by the world's censure or its praise.

Wherever he went impromptu receptions were held in his honor; and we had the privilege of meeting him after our musical; but I had small hope of being received otherwise than in the conventional manner by so great a poet. To my astonishment, however, Mr. Bryant warmly grasped my hand; and said a few words in commendation of my verses, urging me to press bravely on in my work as teacher and writer. By those few words he did inestimable good to a young girl, who had not dared even fancy that she would be able to touch the robe of such a great poetic genius.

From the pleasant recollection of Bryant, I turn to a far different, though also a very kindly man, Horace Greeley. In some respects he was the most remarkable person I have known, because of his personal eccentricities and because of his natural brilliance. Yet he was not always at his best as a conversationalist; and I am free to say that my introduction to him was by no means under favorable circumstances. I was invited to a New Year's party in 1844 at which many notable guests were to be present, but expectation centered around Mr. Greeley; and when he was announced I believe that I actually held my breath, so great was my eagerness.

But instead of the brilliant and genial editor I found him cool and laconic; and very soon he bade us good evening. When I informed our hostess, who was a good friend of mine, that I was rather disappointed in Mr. Greeley, she laughed, and the incident passed; but within five months I was given a delightful chance to change my opinion of the great editor and founder of the "New York Tribune." We again met in the same drawing room as before and many of the guests were the same—but Mr. Greeley was completely transformed; at least he seemed so to me. For the entire evening he was the center of an attentive company, and everyone wanted his opinion on a great variety of subjects. His answers were direct and simple, with no parade of wisdom; no consciousness on his part of intellectual superiority; and music, art and politics, in fact nearly every department of human knowledge or of human endeavor, seemed to interest him and to share his own wit.

The second meeting with Horace Greeley taught me that first impressions, although they are sometimes most lasting, yet often are most unjust. This was my thought as I returned homeward after enjoying the sparkle of Horace Greeley's wit, and I was willing to crown his brow with fadeless laurels.

We also had the privilege of listening to some of the world's greatest singers. Jenny Lind came to our school, taking us by surprise; and for three-quarters of an hour she charmed us with such music as I never heard before, or since, nor do I hope to listen to such melodies again until I hear the choirs of the eternal city.

The year before, that is, 1843, one of the great New York newspapers had offered a prize for the best poem on any subject that one chose to select. Some of my indulgent friends persuaded me to enter the competition, and I chose to write a tribute to Jenny Lind. My friend Bayard Taylor won the

prize; but I believe I won as great an honor; and I
know an honor more pleasing to me, in being permitted to deliver my poem in the presence of Jenny
Lind herself; for, when she came to visit us, I
welcomed the "Swedish Nightingale" in the following stanzas:

We ask no more why strains like thine
  Enchant a listening throng,
For we have felt in one sweet hour
  The magic of thy song.

How like the carol of a bird,
  It stole upon my ear!
Then tenderly it died away
  In echoes soft and clear.

But hark! again its music breaks
  Harmonious on the soul;
How thrills the heart, at every tone,
  With bliss beyond control!

If strains like these, so pure and sweet,
  To mortal lips be given,
What must the glorious anthems be
  Which angels wake in heaven?

'Tis past; 'tis gone. That fairy dream
  Of happiness is o'er;
And we the music of thy voice
  Perhaps may hear no more.

Yet, Sweden's daughter, thou shalt live
  In every grateful heart;
And may the choicest gifts of heaven
  Be thine, where'er thou art.

Among the singers who came a number of times were Adeline Patti and Clara Louise Kellogg; and the visit of Madam LeGrange, while she was in America on a special tour, was also a notable event. Madam LeGrange was asked to sing in the chorus of "Stabat Mater." In the midst of one of the solos she burst into tears because of her sympathy for our pupils in what she took to be a great affliction; but, with a noble effort, she suppressed her emotion, lest she might injure the feelings of those who were sensitive; and thereby won our hearty admiration.

In the midst of these pleasant surroundings my muse occasionally plumed herself for a flight. "The Blind Girl and Other Poems" had been so cordially received by the public that my friends urged me to publish another book; but, in view of the fact that my health for five or six years had been somewhat impaired, such a task seemed out of the question. A number of public occasions, however, had called for special efforts on my part with the result that another volume of poems was collected and published in 1851. The first piece, which gave the title to the book, was called "Monterey"; and it was a long-spun poem, the chief merit of which is a few sincere words of dedication to three of my friends, Mr. Murray, Dr. Clements, and Mr. Chamberlain. Now as I realize that these three dear men have passed beyond the sound of human voices the remembrance of their many kind acts is sweetened and deepened as I recall my early tributes to them; and these flowers of memory are still fadeless and fragrant.

13

A Lesson In Self-Reliance

There is still another man, famous in the annals of our nation, whom I am proud to count among my friends, and now while I write of him the tide of memory turns again bearing me backward more than fifty years on its tranquil bosom, and recalling a lesson in self reliance that he taught me. One morning in 1853, the late Mr. William Cleveland, our principal teacher, came to my classroom and said,

"I have a favor to ask of you. My brother, as you may know, has been appointed secretary to the superintendent. But the death of our father grieves him very much; and when you are at leisure I wish you would speak to him and try to divert his mind from sad thoughts. You can comfort him better than I can." And I promised to do my best.

That afternoon I went into the office and there found Grover Cleveland, a young man of about seventeen, engaged in his work as private secretary.

We exchanged a few sentences and I agreed to come again the next day; for from that hour that we first met a friendship sprang up between us, the links of which must have been woven by angel fingers.

During the hours in which he was not engaged with his office work, he was in the habit of writing my poems as I dictated them to him. Mr. Chamberlain, my old friend, already frequently mentioned, was not superintendent then; but, in his stead, we had a man who expected that all due deference should be paid to himself. Not that he did not wish Mr. Cleveland to copy my verses, but rather that he thought any request should be made through him. At that time, however, I was thirty-five years of age and employed as preceptress at the Institution; and felt, therefore, that I was entitled to the privilege of making my own requests, whenever and of whomsoever I wished, provided that I was not breaking any of the rules or customs of the school.

But, much as I felt this, I hardly dared assert my rights in the matter: and so I said nothing one afternoon when the superintendent came in and forbade me to call on my young amanuensis without consulting him. After he had gone "Grove"—as we then called him—turned to me and said,

"How long are you going to let that man trample on your feelings in this manner?"

"What shall I do?" I asked. He laughed and replied,

"You are certainly within your own rights. So, if you have a poem to be copied tomorrow, come down here, and exactly the same scene will occur as has occurred today. Then, you will have an opportunity to give him as good as he sends; and if you have never learned the lesson of self-reliance, you certainly cannot learn it earlier."

The next day I returned to have some copying done, my little speech all ready; and when the superintendent again objected I "asserted my rights," with the result that he hastily retreated leaving the field in our possession; and so it remained from that time.

Mr. Cleveland and I were constantly associated in our work for more than a year; then he left the Institution; and our paths diverged; but my interest in him has never waned, and I have watched his career with unusual pleasure; not that I was in the least surprised, for all of us expected noble things from him; but because of my own personal regard for his many excellent traits of character. Some years ago I called at his home in Lakewood, New Jersey, and we spent a delightful hour, reviewing the memories of the New York of fifty years ago. In honor of their daughter Ruth I recited the following poem to Mr. and Mrs. Cleveland:

Like the lily bells that blossom
   In the bowers of Eden fair,
All their pretty leaves unfolding
   To the breeze that murmurs there,
Like a jewel bright and sparkling
   From the peerless brow of truth,
Like a birdling with the autumn,
   Came your winsome baby Ruth.

There are feelings deep and tender,
    There are joys you could not know
Till a cherub in your household
    Bade the hidden fountains flow.
Now, a love its smile reflecting
    From the peaceful eye of truth,
Like a radiant star is shining
    O'er your gentle baby Ruth.

In a fancied dream I linger,
    As the evening time draws nigh,
And I listen to the carol
    Of her mamma's lullaby,
While her papa, grave and thoughtful,
    As in years of vanished youth,
Lays his hand with fond caressing
    On the head of baby Ruth.

By a holy consecration
    That will ne'er forgotten be,
You have answered him who whispered
    'Bring your little ones to me.'
You have brought her, pure and lovely,
    To the way, the life, the truth,
And His seal is on the forehead
    Of your precious baby Ruth.

May you train her in the knowledge
    And the wisdom of the Lord,
May you teach her to be faithful,
    And obedient to his word.
With the lamp, whose beams are kindled
    At the throne of sacred truth,
May you guide the coming future
    Of your darling baby Ruth.

In March, 1903, a man professing to be a friend of
mine wrote to Mr. Cleveland to the effect that it
would be a pleasure to hand me a birthday letter if
he would be kind enough to write one. This was
done, but the professed friend sold the ex-President's
note to a newspaper, and the first that I heard of it
was when a reporter called to see if the letter was
genuine. Another copy was sent to me directly
through the mail; and I am glad to quote from it:

"As an old friend," says Mr. Cleveland, "it is a
great pleasure to congratulate you on your coming
birthday, which marks so many years of usefulness
and duty. I am rejoiced to know that your character
and work are amply appreciated by good, kind friends,
who stand about you in your advancing years to
cheer and comfort you. I remember our association
fifty years ago; and it gratifies me to say that you,
who have brought cheer and comfort to so many in
the past, richly deserve now the greatest amount of
grateful acknowledgement, and all the rich recompense, which the love of friends and the approval of
God can supply."

When plans were being made to celebrate my
eighty-fifth birthday in March, 1905, Mr. Cleveland
wrote another beautiful letter, the text of which
follows:

My dear friend:
    It is more than fifty years ago that our acquain-

tance and friendship began; and ever since that
time I have watched your continuous and disinter-
ested labor in uplifting humanity, and pointing out
the way to an appreciation of God's goodness and
mercy.

Though these labors have, I know, brought you
abundant rewards in your consciousness of good
accomplished, those who have known of your works
and sympathized with your noble purposes owe it
to themselves that you are apprized of their remembrance of these things. I am, therefore, exceedingly
gratified to learn that your eighty-fifth birthday is
to be celebrated with a demonstration of this remembrance. As one proud to call you an old friend,
I desire to be early in congratulating you on your
long life of usefulness, and wishing you in the years
yet to be added to you, the peace and comfort born
of the love of God.

Yours very sincerely,

Grover Cleveland

These letters from my friend I prize among my
most valued treasures; and of all the great men in
public life whom I have had the good fortune to
know, I consider him to be one of the greatest; and
in my affection and esteem he holds a place that no
other statesman could possibly occupy.

14

Early Songs and Hymns

In 1845 Mr. George F. Root began to give instruction in music at the Institution; already he was well known as the composer of many sweet hymns and various secular pieces that were exceedingly popular. He used to play many of his melodies for me; and frequently asked me to write words for them. One day in 1851 he played an air that was wonderfully sweet and touching; and I exclaimed.

"Oh, Mr. Root, why don't you publish that?"

"I have no words for it," he replied, "and cannot purchase any." I suggested that he let me try to write something; he assented; and I composed a song beginning as follows:

O come to the greenwood, where nature is smiling,
Come to the greenwood, so lovely and gay,
There will soft music thy spirit beguiling
Tenderly carol thy sadness away.

127

Our first joint composition was a song, entitled "Fare Thee Well, Kitty Dear," which described the grief of a colored man on the death of his beloved; and the chorus runs like this,

Fare thee well, Kitty dear,
Thou art sleeping in thy grave so low,
Nevermore, Kitty dear,
Wilt thou listen to my old banjo.

During the next three years we composed fifty or sixty songs, some of the titles of which are "Bird of the North," "Hazel Dell," "They Have Sold Me Down the River," "O How Glad to Get Home," "Rosalie the Prairie Flower" and "There's Music in the Air."

The success of the concerts given by William B. Bradbury at the Broadway Tabernacle inspired Mr. Root to attempt something in the same manner; and accordingly in 1853 we wrote "The Flower Queen," a cantata, the story of which is as follows: an old man becoming tired of the world, decides to become a hermit; but, as he is about to retire to his lonely hut, he hears a chorus singing, "Who shall be queen of the flowers?" His interest is at once aroused; and on the following day he is asked to act as judge in a contest where each flower urges her claims to be queen of all the others. At length the hermit chooses the rose for her loveliness; and in turn she exhorts him to return to the world and to his duty.

I believe that "The Flower Queen" was the first American cantata; and it was immediately in great demand. It was followed by the "Pilgrim Fathers," for which Dr. Lowell Mason assisted in composing the music.

On March 2, 1858, I left the New York Institution for the Blind; and my parting from those familiar surroundings was indeed sad; for I had been nearly twenty-three years, eight as a pupil, and fifteen as a teacher. Prior to this I had written no hymns, except possibly one or two short religious poems that may have been set to music; but I had been engaged in writing verses and short prose sketches for several papers. The best of my work had been collected into three books, although the great bulk of personal and miscellaneous pieces were never gathered together; and I am indeed glad that they were not. The third book of poems was compiled a few months after I left the Institution, under the title of "A Wreath of Columbia's Flowers"; and it suffered more than the others from the need of careful pruning and revision.

In 1858 I was married to Mr. Alexander Van Alstyne whom I had known as pupil and teacher in the Institution for almost fifteen years. By nature he was endowed with superior musical ability; and, before he graduated from our school, he was said to be one of the most accomplished students that we

ever had there. He continued his education in Union College, where in addition to music he studied
classics and theology; and then he taught at Albion,
New York, until 1855 when he returned to teach in
our school, which he continued to do, with rare
skill and sympathy with his pupils for three years.

After our marriage he insisted that my literary
name should remain as it had become known to the
public in general through my poems. Our tastes
were congenial and he composed the music to several of my hymns besides constantly aiding me
with kind criticism and advice. At different times
he was organist in two of the New York churches;
and also taught private classes in both vocal and
instrumental music. He was a firm, trustful Christian and a man whose kindly deeds and cheering
words will not be forgotten by his many friends. We
were happy together many years. His death occurred
on July 18, 1902.

As early as 1860 the name of William B. Bradbury
was familiar to all lovers of music. To the Christian
world he was known principally as the author of a
large collection of sweet melodies, many of which
have found their way into the best collection of
hymns. Prior to 1864 I had never met this gifted
composer; but I had often fancied that our tastes
might be congenial; and, on this account, I was
somewhat anxious to make his acquaintance. The
opportunity to do so soon came through the Rev.
Peter Stryker, the minister of the Dutch Reformed
Church in Twenty-third Street, which I frequently
attended. In December, 1863, Mr. Stryker asked me

to write a short poem that could be used as a hymn in the closing services of the year. Early in January he came to me and said,

"Why don't you see Mr. Bradbury? He has told me more than once that he was looking for someone who could write hymns. I think you are the person for whom he has been looking and I will give you a letter of introduction."

In consequence of this arrangement, on February 2, 1864, I presented myself at the office of William B. Bradbury, 425 Broome Street. To my surprise Mr. Bradbury said,

"Fanny, I thank God that we have at last met; for I think you can write hymns; and I have wished for a long time to have a talk with you." At the end of a brief interview I promised to bring him something before the week drew to a close; and three days later I returned with some verses that were soon set to music and published as my first hymn. There were four stanzas; and three of them I will quote here:

> We are going, we are going
>   To a home beyond the skies,
> Where the fields are robed in beauty,
>   And the sunlight never dies;
>
> Where the fount of joy is flowing
>   In the valley green and fair.
> We shall dwell in love together;
>   There shall be no parting there.
>
> We are going, we are going,
>   And the music we have heard,

Like the echo of the woodland,
Or the carol of a bird.

The following week Mr. Bradbury sent for me in
great haste; and said that he wanted a patriotic song
at once. As a title he chose "A Sound Among the
Mulberry Trees"; but I timidly suggested that "Forest Trees" would be more euphonious, to which
idea he at once assented. The melody that he had
composed was somewhat difficult; but, having heard
it two or three times, I was able to count the
measure, and the words were then easily adapted.
On the following morning I carried the song to the
office of Mr. Bradbury, but he was not there; and so
his bookkeeper, who was also a musical man, played
it on the piano, exclaiming, "How in the world did
you manage to write that hymn? Nobody ever supposed that you, or any other mortal, could adapt
words to that melody."

At this moment Mr. Bradbury entered the office;
and after looking over the hymn very carefully,
turned to me and exclaimed,

"Fanny, I am surprised beyond measure; and, now,
let me say that as long as I have a publishing house,
you will always have work." The future verified his
promise, for I have been with Mr. Bradbury and his
successors, the Biglow and Main Company, more
than forty years.

15

The Life of a Hymn-Writer

The song "There Is a Sound Among the Forest Trees" was used during the Civil War; but after that cruel conflict was over I said to Mr. Bradbury,

"What are you going to do with 'Forest Trees'?"

"What can we do with it?" he asked.

"Oh," I replied, "we can write sacred words to the melody; and indeed the subject comes to me now: 'There's A Cry from Macedonia.'" With his permission I composed a missionary hymn that was very popular for many years; and thus my life as a writer of gospel hymns began under most favorable circumstances.

Sometimes Mr. Bradbury gave me the titles for hymns to melodies already written; but more often I was allowed to make my own selection; and a part of my duties was to revise poems that Mr. Bradbury had already secured from other authors. During a period of four years we worked side by side, until, at length, in April, 1866, he was taken very ill; and the following winter was obliged to go South for three months. At the end of this period he returned greatly benefited by the change, but all of his associates at the office were reluctantly forced to admit that consumption was slowly wearing his life away. Yet his vitality and heroic resistance were wonderful; and he was able to compose many beautiful melodies.

One afternoon, in the autumn of 1867, he called me to him and said,

"These interviews have been very pleasant to me, but they will soon be over; I am going to be forever with the Lord; and I will await you on the bank of the river."

I was greatly moved by his words, and cried,

"Oh, must I lose a friendship that I have enjoyed so much?"

"No," replied he, "take up my lifework where I lay it down; and you will not indeed lose a friendship, though I am going away from you, but rather strengthen it by striving to carry out my own ideals."

At a cloudless sunset, January 7, 1868, Mr. Bradbury passed away. The children always loved him dearly; and on the day of his funeral they brought a wreath of oak leaves and laid it tenderly upon his casket. To me the sad occasion was the more memorable because the first hymn that we wrote together was sung during the service; but the lines of my own production brought comfort to my aching heart, when I realized what a friend had passed to his reward, and that he had gone to that country

> Where the fields are robed in beauty,
> And the sunlight never dies.

I met Theodore E. Perkins in June, 1864, and also
Philip Phillips about the same time. The first hymn
that I wrote for Mr. Perkins was:

> I know thou art praying tonight, mother,
> I know thou art praying for me.

Mr. Bradbury introduced me to Philip Phillips at
the store; he had come from Cincinnati; and already knew me somewhat by reputation. As they
were going through the store, Mr. Phillips said,
laughingly, "Fanny, I wish you would write me a
hymn, and have it ready when we return." "This is
Mr. Bradbury's time," said I, "and will you ask his
permission?" Mr. Bradbury said,
"Oh, Fanny, that is all right." So I wrote three or
four stanzas while they were gone; Mr. Phillips
liked them very much; and from that time often
called on me for hymns to use in his evangelistic
meetings.

In 1866 Mr. Phillips published a collection of
hymns called the "Singing Pilgrim"; and while he
was preparing that book he sent me forty titles to
which I composed words and not a single poem was

written by my amanuensis until the whole number
was completed. They were then forwarded to Mr.
Phillips at Cincinnati; he again sent me a long list
of titles and they were treated exactly as the first
forty had been. This incident is not told to commend myself, but merely to illustrate to what extent memory will serve us, if we only give memory
a fair chance. The mind appears to me like a great
storehouse into which we place various articles for
safekeeping and sometimes even forget that they
are there, but, sooner or later, we find them; and so
I lay aside my intellectual wares for some future day
or need; and in the meantime often forget them,
until the call comes for a hymn.

Shortly after the death of Mr. Bradbury the firm
of Biglow and Main was organized. Of Sylvester
Main I have already spoken and told the story of our
meeting thirty-five years after we had known each
other in Ridgefield. From his sixteenth year he had
been a singing teacher and a well known chorister
in Norfolk Street Methodist Church in New York
City. Two years, or more, previous to my meeting
with him at the office of Mr. Bradbury, he had been
associated in the publishing business, and he continued as a member of the firm until his lamented
death in 1873; and I always found him a faithful
counsellor and a friend whose memory I highly
prize. His last words were,

"The dear Lord is about to give me rest. If you
love me, do not weep, but rejoice." These words of
cheer, coming as the parting message of one whom
I had loved, in after years proved a source of inspira-

tion and comfort in many an hour of depression; and the words of one of my own hymns, for which his son, Hubert P. Main, wrote beautiful music often recall sweet memories of him, and many other friends, who await me in the Better Land:

> On the banks beyond the river
> We shall meet no more to sever,
> In the bright, the bright forever,
> In the summerland of song.

L. H. Biglow, the senior member of the firm, continued the publishing business after the death of Mr. Main. For thirty years we were constantly associated together, and during this time not the slightest misunderstanding arose between us, so that, although not now connected with the firm, he still remains my trusted friend as in the days when we more frequently met. Hubert P. Main I have known since 1866, and he has always been of valuable service to me in criticising my work, for which his knowledge of hymns, both ancient and modern, has well fitted him. His musical library has been the scene of many pleasant talks concerning the writing of hymns and their accompanying melodies. For many years he has been the accomplished compiler for the Biglow and Main Company, and he has set to music some of my best hymns, including such favorites as "The Bright Forever," "Hold Thou My Hand," "Blessed Homeland," "The Blessed Rock," "Yes, There's Pardon for You," and many others.

Previous to 1870 the Biglow and Main hymns were widely known in several foreign countries, especially in England. Our publishing house was the rendezvous of a company of musical men, who were in the habit of meeting together after the publication of a new book, for the purpose of singing it through from cover to cover. Among these musical friends may be mentioned Hubert P. Main, William F. Sherwin, Theodore F. Seward, Henry Tucker, Chester G. Allen, Philip Phillips and Theodore E. Perkins, but of this merry group Mr. Main and Mr. Perkins are all that now survive.

From 1872 until the time of her death, seven years later, Frances Ridley Havergal and I corresponded at frequent intervals, and she wrote me a poem of tribute, an extract from which will be found later in this book, together with an account of the incident that led her to thus remember me.

My recollection of Rev. Dr. Robert Lowry dates from 1866. The first hymn of mine for which he composed the music was "All the Way My Savior Leads Me." He used to read to us selections from favorite authors during the long summer afternoons, and I well remember his reading Browning's "Rabbi ben Ezra" a poem of which he was very fond, and how it reminded us all of the good doctor himself.

Grow old along with me, the best is yet to be,
The last of life for which the first was planned.

As a critic Dr. Lowry was possessed of excellent taste, and we never so much as thought of appealing from any decision of his whenever the question in dispute related either to poetry or music, for his ear was trained to detect the most minute metrical fault. In 1897 he assisted me in the selection of my best hymns and poems for a book called "Bells at Evening" for which he wrote a very sympathetic biographical introduction from material mostly furnished by Hubert P. Main.

Ere long, however, Dr. Lowry's health began to fail and we watched him with growing anxiety. I shall always recall our last meeting at his home in Plainfield, New Jersey, with tender emotions. We talked together of many of the events of thirty years, and finally he said,

"Fanny, I am going to join those who have gone before, for my work is now done." I could not speak with him concerning the parting without betraying my grief, so I simply took his hand in mind and said quietly,

"I thank you, Doctor Lowry, for all that you have done for me; good night, until we meet in the morning." Then I silently went down the stairs, with the impression on my mind that the good man would soon be at rest from his labors, and so indeed it proved.

A little while to weep for those we cherish,
As one by one they near the river's brink;
A little while to catch their sweet assurance,
That we in heaven shall find each missing link;

A little while and then the glorious dawning
Of that fair morn beyond the swelling tide,
When we shall wake and in our Savior's likeness,
Perfect and pure, we shall be satisfied.

Although some of my most treasured friends have passed beyond the sound of human voices, others there are who remain to add their graceful benediction to a life full of blessings and already crowned with peace.

In the year 1867 I met Dr. William H. Doane under very interesting circumstances. He had come from his home in Cincinnati to New York to visit his friend Dr. Van Meter of the Five Points Mission; and they were looking for a hymn that might be used on a certain anniversary. A number of standard hymns were given to Mr. Doane, but he did not find them appropriate. About this time I had been writing "More Like Jesus"; and Dr. Lowry asked me why I did not send it to Mr. Doane. I said, "Well, I will" and accordingly sent it by a messenger boy. The latter handed my words to Mr. Doane, who happened to be at the moment talking with Dr. Van Meter; and he laid them down for a few minutes. When he took up the letter and glanced over its contents he started after the boy, but could not find him. He returned to Dr. Van Meter disheartened, but determined to find me if I was anywhere to be found in the city. He again went out and hunted for me the rest of the day; and it was not until about eight or nine in the evening that he was finally

Fanny Crosby and her husband

directed to my boarding place. I went to the door, and he asked, "Are you Fanny Crosby?" On being informed I was that person he said,

"Oh, how glad I am to find you; I have been trying to do so a long while, and at last I have succeeded." At the close of our interview he said,

"I must pay you for the hymn that you sent and which I was more than glad to receive." He put into my hand what he supposed to be a two-dollar bill, and then bade me good night. It struck me that I ought to ask him how much he had given me; that there might be no mistake about it. He came back; I showed him the bill, which proved to be twenty dollars. Of course, I declined to take that amount; but he said that the Lord had sent that hymn, and therefore meant that I should have the twenty dollars for it. The following evening he renewed his visit and gave me the subject "Pass Me Not, O Gentle Savior."

Meanwhile Dr. Van Meter had called on Mr. Doane, and finding that he had not been able to compose a melody for the anniversary at the mission, said

"Here is another piece; I will come tomorrow and shall expect the music to be written." Mr. Doane took up my hymn "More Like Jesus" and the melody came to him at once. According to promise his friend came again next day and said, "Is the piece ready?" Mr. Doane said,

"Not the music to the words you gave yesterday, but I have something else; and if we can find an organ I will play it for you." They went into a neighboring church, and Dr. Van Meter agreed to pump the organ while Mr. Doane played and sang the hymn. But they had not gone very far before Dr. Van Meter burst into tears and forgot to pump the organ. They tried again, and this time the good doctor came out from behind the organ, threw his arms around Mr. Doane's neck and cried,

"Doane, where did you get that?" Then Mr. Doane told him that Fanny Crosby had sent him the words and he had just written the music. The hymn was used at the anniversary and was a perfect success.

16

Two Great Evangelists

In the thought of Christian people everywhere throughout the world the names, Moody and Sankey, are linked together; and I have been not a little honored in having these great evangelists among my dearest friends. I have always been greatly fascinated when Mr. Sankey has related in my hearing the story of how he and Mr. Moody first met; and he has told it with wonderful vividness and power in his "Story of the Gospel Hymns." In 1870 Mr. Sankey was one of the delegates to the convention of the Young Men's Christian Association at Indianapolis; and one morning, with a friend, went into a seven o'clock meeting conducted by Mr. Moody. The singing was abominable and the friend suggested that Mr. Sankey start something; and he sang "There Is a Fountain Filled with Blood." The congregation joined and the remainder of the meeting was bright and hearty.

At the conclusion of the service they met, and

Fanny Crosby and Mr. Sankey at work fitting words and music

Mr. Moody's first words were, "I have been looking for you for the last eight years. You must come to Chicago and help me in my evangelistic meetings." This announcement was rather sudden; and Mr. Sankey replied that he did not feel called to give up his business, but promised to think the matter over. The next day Mr. Moody asked him to be at a certain street corner that evening. He arrived before the evangelist; the latter soon came; and without even greeting Mr. Sankey passed into a store and asked for a box upon which he might stand and speak to the men returning home from work. A large company collected; they at last adjourned to the Opera House, where the convention was being held; and continued the meeting till the hour of the evening service. For the next six months Mr. Moody urged Mr. Sankey to give up his business and go to Chicago; finally he was promised that they would hold a few meetings together; and before the end of the first week Mr. Sankey sent his resignation to his firm. Thus early in 1871 they began work. Wherever Moody and Sankey went there was a great awakening, and in England especially thousands turned toward the Christian life from a career of indifference and sin. Mr. Sankey was in the habit of using some of the songs which had proved their merit in Chicago and other cities of America, but the demand for gospel hymns rose to such a degree that a collection of them was printed, and the little book was called "Sacred Songs and Solos." The sales were constantly increased until many thousands were sold. The profit from the publication was given to charitable purposes.

When they returned to this country a new book was compiled with the assistance of P. P. Bliss and Major D. W. Whittle. It was entitled "Gospel Hymns and Sacred Songs" and was issued by the Biglow and Main Company. Since that date five additional numbers have been compiled and over fifty million copies in all have been sold, the royalty being devoted to worthy causes, and of late years to the Northfield Seminary and the Boys' School at Mount Hermon, Massachusetts. Recent editions have been compiled by George C. Stebbins and James McGranahan, both of whom have been friends of mine for many years.

I presume "The Ninety and Nine" is the most popular of all the Moody and Sankey hymns. The story of the writing of this hymn has been told to me more than once by Mr. Sankey. They had been traveling through England and Scotland, holding very large meetings, and finally were going from Glasgow to Edinburgh. At the railway station Mr. Sankey purchased a paper with the hope of finding some news from America. He found none, however, but at last caught sight of a little poem in one corner of the paper among the advertisements. He liked it very much, called Mr. Moody's attention to it; and read it again at his friend's request. But Mr. Moody was not impressed. Two days later the topic at a noon meeting was "The Good Shepherd"; and Dr. Bonar was one of the speakers. When he had concluded his address Mr. Moody asked if Mr. Sankey had some solo appropriate to this subject. He had nothing in mind; and was greatly perplexed as to what to do; then a voice seemed to say, "Sing the hymn you found on the train." He immediately sat down at the organ; bowed his head in prayer; and at once the music to "The Ninety and Nine" came as it now stands. The great audience was deeply touched.

Several interesting stories have grown out of the singing of "The Ninety and Nine" on special occasions. Many years ago there lived at Northfield an infidel; and one day, while all the neighbors had gone to the meeting at the church, he sat at home alone feeling dissatisfied with himself and all the world in general. But he heard Mr. Sankey singing "The Ninety and Nine"; and there was something in the hymn that he could not escape. The melody rang in his ears, and the thought of the lost sheep troubled him that night, and the next, and the following day until the evening, when he could stand it no longer. He went to the meeting and returned a saved man.

A few years later he was taken ill. One day he said to his wife,

"Raise the window; I hear 'The Ninety and Nine.'" Then he listened attentively until the last notes of the hymn had died out; and turned from the window he said,

"I am dying; but it is all right, for I am ready. I shall never hear 'The Ninety and Nine' again on earth, but I am glad that I have heard it once more today."

My own recollections of Northfield bring back

many incidents concerning those whom it was my
fortune to meet there. During the summer of 1894
the auditorium meetings were in charge of Dr. A. J.
Gordon, while Mr. Moody was holding a series of
evangelistic services in England. One evening Mr.
Sankey came to me and said,

"Will you say something? There is a request from
the audience that you speak." I felt that I was not
prepared for the occasion and so I said,

"Oh, Mr. Sankey, I cannot speak before such an
array of talent." Dr. Pierson supplemented Mr.
Sankey's request by saying,

"Yes, you can. There is no one here of whom you
need be afraid." Then Dr. Gordon said,

"Fanny, do you speak to please man or to please
God?"

"Why, I hope to please God," I replied. "Well,
then," he said, "go out and do your duty."

During my remarks that evening I repeated for
the first time in public the words to "Saved by
Grace," although the hymn had been written more
than two years before that summer, but it had never
been published or used in any way.

"Where have you kept that piece?" asked Mr.
Sankey, when I returned to my seat. I told him that
I had kept it stored away for an emergency. There
was a reporter present that evening; he copied the
hymn as I gave it; and a few weeks later it appeared
in an English religious paper. At the request of Mr.
Sankey, my friend, George C. Stebbins, composed
the music to "Saved by Grace" and thus the hymn
was sent forth on its mission to the world.

So strong was the friendship existing between Mr. Moody and Mr. Sankey that we used to call them "David and Jonathan"; and I am sure that the modern church has not known two men more devoted to the work of Christian evangelism; and so they went far and near, telling the old, old story in sermon and in gospel song, until the influence of their meetings spread through all classes of society.

My last personal message from Mr. Moody was received shortly before his death while I was conducting a series of meetings in Oneonta, New York. A friend of mine was leaving for Northfield; and at my request he carried a message of greeting to Mr. Moody; and when the latter heard it, he exclaimed, "Oh, Fanny Crosby, give her my love." I little thought then that before many months the sender of those kind words would sleep on the summit of old Round Top, where we had gathered many beautiful summer evenings to hear his words of comfort and of inspiration.

Dwight Lyman Moody was a wonderful man; and he did his own work in a unique way, which was sometimes no less daring than original. The following passage from the Holy Book is in my mind as I think of his blameless life:

"Blessed are the dead which die in the Lord from henceforth. Yea, saith the Spirit, that they may rest from their labors, and their works do follow them."

It is a blessed joy that his companion, Mr. Sankey, has been spared to the present hour; and that during the last twenty-five years he has been a close associate of mine in writing gospel hymns. His work as a composer and as a singer is known throughout the length and breadth of the Christian world; for the sorrowing and unfortunate of both America and Great Britain he has done an amount of good that eternity alone will be able to estimate; and his own sweet melodies have indeed been a balm to many an aching heart.

The friendship of this talented man is one of my priceless jewels. During a recent illness I told him that I believed the entire Christian world was praying for his recovery. He said, "Tell those who love me and are praying for me that I am holding on to Christ and Christ is holding on to me; and that by and by I'll see Him face to face and tell the story 'Saved by Grace.'"

Recently while visiting at Mr. Sankey's home, I heard him calling from his room upstairs, "Fanny Crosby is in this house; I hear her laugh." Then I went to his room; we conversed pleasantly for a long time; and the next day when I was leaving his home he handed me the following hymn, saying "You may have this for your book." The words were written by Sarah Dougney, and set to music composed by himself.

Sleep on, beloved, sleep, and take thy rest;
Lay down thy head upon thy Savior's breast;
We loved thee well, but Jesus loves thee best—
    Good-night! Good-night!

Calm is thy slumber as an infant's sleep;
But thou shall wake no more to toil and weep:

This is a perfect rest, secure, and deep—
  Good-night! Good-night!

Until the shadows from this earth are cast;
Until he gathers in his sheaves at last;
Until the twilight gloom be overpast—
  Good-night! Good-night!

Until the Easter glory lights the skies;
Until the dead in Jesus shall arise,
And he shall come, but not in lowly guise—
  Good-night! Good-night!

Until made beautiful by love divine,
Thou in the likeness of thy Lord shalt shine,
And he shall bring that golden crown of thine—
  Good-night! Good-night!

Only "Good-night," beloved—not "farewell!"
A little while, and all his saints shall dwell
In hallowed union indivisible—
  Good-night! Good-night!

Until we meet again before his throne,
Clothed in the spotless robe he gives his own,
Until we know even as we are known—
  Good-night! Good-night!

Then he gave me a message for the same purpose. "I wish you to convey to all my friends," said Mr. Sankey, "the assurance of my love; and that I hope to meet them all by-and-by in the land where there is no more sorrow nor pain, and where God shall wipe away all tears from our eyes. Tell them that *God is Love* and that I have ordered those words to be cut on my tombstone in Greenwood, that future generations may know the faith in which I died."

Later he wrote:

Dear Fanny, co-laborer in the blessed service of sacred song for so many years:

I wish that when you get to heaven (as you may before I will) that you will watch for me at the pearly gate at the eastern side of the city; and when I get there I'll take you by the hand and lead you along the golden street, up to the throne of God, and there we'll stand before the lamb, and say to him: And now we see thee face to face, saved by thy matchless, boundless grace, and we are satisfied.

Yours, till the day dawn and the shadows flee away,

Ira D. Sankey

(17)

Other Literary and Musical Friendships

In general I have been always willing to agree with authors as to the merits of their own poems. That often is the safer plan, and in the end may save a vast deal of ill feeling. One funny instance comes to mind now. Fifty or more years ago I knew a man who thought he had a genius for poetry; and when I was calling at his house he recited one of his own productions, of which I recall only this stanza:

> I am what is called a sinner
> By those who think they are right;
> But then I hope to go where
> The blind receive their sight.

I said, "Why, Mr. Brown, did you write that?" endeavoring to look as demure as possible. He seemed to be much flattered, and said, "I have been thinking that you and I could write a book together."

Summoning all the gravity I could, I exclaimed, "Wouldn't that be splendid!" The book, however, was never written.

An irregular line frequently makes a poem unsuited to music. In my work I have seldom undertaken even the slightest revision in the poems of others, without being perfectly sure that it was wished. Once, when I departed from this rule, to gratify the wish of the editor of a certain New York magazine, I repented at leisure. Someone had sent in a piece entitled "Charlie and I"; I revised it; and a few days after the magazine was published the author came down to interview me. Not until some time later did she become fully reconciled and then only through the friendly offices of my colleague, the late Mrs. Mary A. Kidder. Then we became firm friends; but the lesson taught me by such an unpleasant incident has saved me from like repetitions.

Miss Josephine Pollard and Mrs. Kidder also wrote many hymns for Mr. Bradbury, and his successors, the Biglow and Main Company; and the three of us worked together so well that they were in the habit of calling us "the trio."

Philip P. Bliss was introduced to me in 1874. His talent for music was inherited, though his early advantages were few. When he was ten years of age he heard a piano for the first time; and, becoming enraptured by the music, he sought the source of it which proved to be the parlor of an entire stranger. But the boy was so enchanted that he did not think of that; and so entered; and there found a young lady seated at the piano, but she ordered him out.

This same boy, however, mostly through his own
efforts, had become so proficient in music, after a
very few years that he was asked to lead large
chorus classes.

The death of Mr. Bliss at the beginning of what
seemed a career of great promise cast a cloud over
the spirits of all his friends. The night before that
terrible railroad accident at Ashtabula, Ohio, in
which he lost his life in a vain attempt to save that
of his beloved wife, he said to his audience, "I may
not pass this way again"; then he sang a solo, "I'm
Going Home Tomorrow." This indeed proved pro-
phetic of his own home going.

His celebrated hymn "Hold the Fort" was born
one day in the summer of 1870, while he and Major
Whittle were attending a meeting at Rockford, Illi-
nois; and it was first used at the Young Men's
Christian Association in Chicago. Mr. Bliss was
inspired to write his hymn by a story told by Major
Whittle. My last meeting with the latter seems but
yesterday. He was suffering much pain, and I said,
"Oh, major, I wish I could give you a part of my
good health this morning." The dear, patient man
replied, "It is all right. The Lord knows best; and all
will result in my good." Then he spoke pleasantly
of some favorite hymns, and added with a smile,
"All sorrow will fade away, and all pain depart as the
dew before the morning sun."

There are many other musical men whom I have
had the honor of knowing and whom I number
among my dearest acquaintances. I met Hart P.
Danks and William F. Sherwin about the same year;

D. Horatio R. Palmer has entertained us many an afternoon with his delightful reminiscences of the Holy Land; and Mr. George C. Stebbins, who has written the music to "Saved by Grace," "Eye Hath Not Seen," "Come Unto Me, Ye Weary," "In Perfect Peace," and other famous hymns, is another of my priceless friends.

Some of those who have already crossed to the other side of the river are Victor H. Benke, William B. Bradbury, Philip P. Bliss, George F. Bristow, Henry Brown, Hart P. Danks, Mary A. Kidder, Robert Lowry, Sylvester Main, Philip Phillips, Josephine Pollard, Henry Tucker, Theodore F. Seward, William F. Sherwin, John R. Sweney, Silas J. Vail, and Mrs. Clark Wilson; a few of the musical associates who are still spared are James M. Black, John R. Clements, Mrs. Mary Upham Currier, William H. Doane, Caryl Florio, Charles H. Gabriel, Adam Geibel, Mrs. Harriet E. Jones, Miss Eliza E. Hewitt, William J. Kirkpatrick, Mrs. Joseph F. Knapp, Hubert P. Main, James McGranahan, H. R. Palmer, Theodore E. Perkins, W. A. Post, Ira D. Sankey, I. Allan Sankey, Mrs. Lanta Wilson Smith, George C. Stebbins, B. C. Unseld, J. W. Vandeventer, W. S. Weeden, Clark Wilson, Mrs. Agnes Woolston and David D. Wood.

I have visited Mr. Kirkpatrick at his home in Philadelphia several times; and I look back on these occasions with peculiar pleasure. To some of the melodies that he has sent I have written words that have been largely used for many years in gospel services everywhere. A few of the titles that come to mind now are "He Hideth My Soul," "He Came to Save Me," "Redeemed," "Welcome for Me," "Meet Me There," and "Like a Bird on the Deep"; and my readers will instantly recall many others, equally popular.

Miss Eliza E. Hewitt, who has written many beautiful hymns and poems for Mr. Kirkpatrick and other composers, several years ago called on me while I was in Philadelphia; and her visit was indeed a gracious benediction. At Assembly Park, New York, recently we renewed the friendship then so favorably begun; and there we spent many delightful hours in conversation about subjects dear to both of us. Miss Hewitt's hymn, entitled "Will There Be Any Stars in My Crown?" is a great favorite of mine. Mrs. Harriet E. Jones, also the author of hundreds of inspiring gospel songs, though I have met her but once, has proved a loving friend in her cheering letters for several years.

How can I fittingly describe my impressions of Ocean Grove? The first evening that I was there was clear calm; and as we silently rowed across Wesley Lake some music from the camp grounds was wafted to us with a delightful cadence. Among the lasting friendships formed at Ocean Grove were those of John R. Sweney and William J. Kirkpatrick.

Shortly after my arrival at Ocean Grove in 1877 I was met by a man, whom I had known in the old Norfolk Street Church in New York. Twelve months before I had seen him under totally different circumstances, so different in fact that his story should be of some interest. Then he was disheartened; now he was thrilled with Christian hope; and we were indeed surprised by the complete transformation. On the evening of our previous meeting he arose and said,

"Friends, I know I have done wrong; and many times I have asked your prayers. But tonight I *must* have your help."

His manner impressed me exceedingly, and I gave him some words of cheer; but the majority of our members had little faith in his reformation, because he had tried so many times and failed. His greeting to me at Ocean Grove was as follows:

"I want to thank you for your kind words in my behalf at the Norfolk Street Church." Some of the most gratifying memories of my life center about testimonies of those whom I have been enabled to help by words of cheer towards better things than those of this world.

Dr. Stokes, who conducted the meetings at Ocean Grove, was a sweet, spiritual man; and he wrote several inspiring hymns, including, "Holy Spirit, Fill Me Now," by which many an audience has been moved to tears as Mr. Sweney sang it as a solo. It was one of the saddest duties of my life to recite a tribute to his memory at a public reception given to Mr. Sweney.

The work of the Christian missionary has always had a fascination for me that all other callings have lacked; and, consequently, it was a rare privilege to sit at the feet of the saintly Bishop William Taylor and hear him tell of the tribes which live where "Afric's sunny fountains pour down their golden sand," as Bishop Heber has said in his great missionary hymn. The good Bishop Taylor bore the heat of the day until his locks were snowy and his strength ebbing fast. On one occasion when he was starting for Africa he said to me,

"Fanny, if you were thirty years younger would you go with me to Africa?"

"Yes indeed, I would," I answered, "and help you plant missions." I saw him again a few weeks before his last missionary journey and he said,

"Well, Fanny, I am going once more."

"Many times yet," said I, "if it be our Father's will." Laying his hand on my head he gave me his blessing; and as he stood there a vision of the multitudes to whom his ministry had been a benediction came before my eyes with a strange power and pathos. My prayer is: May the hour come when we will no longer say of the foreign field, "Lo, the harvest is ripe, but where are the reapers?"

The unique illustrations given by Dr. Talmage always interested me, one of them in particular. In a Christmas sermon he told the story of a little Swiss girl who was dying; and from her window she could look out to the lofty summit of the mountains amid which she had been reared.

"Papa, carry me to the top of the mountain," she exclaimed. But he replied,

"My child, I cannot carry you, but the angels will." For a time she was silent and lay with her eyes closed. At length she opened them and looking out of the window exclaimed in her joy,

"They *are* carrying me, father. I shall soon be at the top."

With those words Dr. Talmage concluded his sermon. It seemed to his hearers that he had conducted them to a high pinnacle in a lofty range of mountains where they might breathe a pure atmosphere. When I reminded him of the beautiful effect that his words had on us, he said,

"Ah, you are right. I never intended to bring you down from that summit."

And thus it is with even the humblest fellow ministers of song; they take us to heights of which the soul often dreams, yet rarely attains, in fact to those mansions of the blest where there are always light and warmth and love; where the thirst of weary pilgrims is quenched by draughts of mountain springs; and where this mortal spirit puts on its immortality.

> Sing on, ye joyful pilgrims,
> The way will not be long,
> My faith is heavenward rising
> With every tuneful song.

18

Work Among Missions

My connection with the Bowery Mission dates from 1881. Mr. Childs, then its superintendent, I first knew as a discouraged man out of work, but always found him a true Christian gentleman. He had been compelled to give up an excellent position in Massachusetts because of failing eyesight; and consequently had come to New York to find something to do. We first met on a street car; and I asked him if he was familiar with the Bowery Mission. He said that he was, and the next evening we went down there together, and I introduced him to the Rev. Mr. Rulifson, the superintendent, with the result that he was at once engaged as assistant in the work of rescuing lost men.

I frequently attended the evening meetings at the mission; and one evening they asked me to speak, as indeed they often did. During my remarks I said,

"If there is a man present, who has gone just as

far as he can go, he is the person with whom I want to shake hands." Mr. Childs whispered,

"The man for whom you are looking sits directly in front of the platform."

When the meeting closed I was introduced to this stranger; and asked him if he did not wish to come out and live a Christian life.

"Oh," he replied, "what difference? I have no friends; nobody cares for me."

"You are mistaken," I said, "for the Lord Jesus cares for you; and others care for you too. Unless I had a deep interest in your soul's welfare I certainly would not be here talking with you on this subject." Then, I gave him several passages of Scripture, for he seemed moved to consider the matter carefully. At last he said,

"If I come here to the meeting tomorrow evening and sign the pledge, will you come with me?" To which question I replied,

"Yes, I will be here again; and, although I do not discourage you from signing the pledge, it seems to me that the best pledge you can give is to yield yourself to God. Will you do it?" The next evening he was present; and before the close of the meeting we saw the new light in his eyes and felt the change in his voice.

Kindness in this world will do much to help others, not only to come into the light, but to grow in grace day by day. There are many timid souls whom we jostle morning and evening as we pass them by; but if only the kind word were spoken they might become fully persuaded. For all mission workers everywhere I always have had tender sympathies. God bless them!

Not a few of my hymns have been written after experiences at the New York missions. One in particular has been used far and wide in evangelistic work. As I was addressing a large company of working men one hot August evening, the thought kept forcing itself on my mind that some mother's boy must be rescued that very night or perhaps not at all. So I requested that, if there was any boy present, who had wandered away from mother's teaching, he would come to the platform at the conclusion of the service. A young man of eighteen came forward and said,

"Did you mean me? I have promised my mother to meet her in heaven; but as I am now living that will be impossible." We prayed for him; he finally arose with a new light in his eyes; and exclaimed triumphantly,

"Now, I can meet mother in heaven; for I have found her God."

A few days before, Mr. Doane had sent me the subject "Rescue the Perishing," and while I sat there that evening the line came to me,

"Rescue the perishing, care for the dying."

I could think of nothing else that night. When I arrived at my home I went to work on it at once; and before I retired the entire hymn was ready for a melody. The next day my words were written and forwarded to Mr. Doane, who wrote the beautiful and touching music as it now stands.

In November, 1903, I went to Lynn, Massachusetts, to speak before the Young Men's Christian Association. I told them the incident that led me to write "Rescue the Perishing," as I have just related it. After the meeting a large number of men shook hands with me, and among them was a man, who seemed to be deeply moved. You may imagine my surprise when he said,

"Miss Crosby, I was the boy, who told you more than thirty-five years ago that I had wandered from my mother's God. The evening that you spoke at the mission I sought and found peace, and I have tried to live a consistent Christian life ever since. If we never meet again on earth, we will meet up yonder." As he said this, he raised my hand to his lips; and before I had recovered from my surprise he had gone; and remains to this day a nameless friend, who touched a deep chord of sympathy in my heart. It is these notes of sympathy that vibrate when a voice calls them forth from the dim memories of the past, and the music is celestial.

One evening there was a man in the seat in front of me, and from his singing I judged that he was under conviction. Something within prompted me to ask him if he would remain and hear the sermon, and he finally consented to do so. Just before the close of the address I whispered,

"When the invitation is given, will you go to the altar?" For a moment he hesitated, and then asked,

"Will you go with me?" I did go to the altar with him and had the pleasure of seeing him a saved man.

I could give more than one instance where men have been reclaimed, after a long struggle and many attempts at reformation, because someone spoke a kind word to them even at what appeared to be the last moment. I have also known many others who turned away from a meeting simply because the cheering word had not been spoken, nor the helping hand extended.

Never to chide the erring has always been my policy, for I firmly believe that harsh words only serve to harden hearts that might otherwise be softened into repentance.

Speak not harshly when reproving
Those from duty's path who stray;
If you would reclaim the erring,
Kindness must each action sway.
Speak not harshly to the wayward;
Win their confidence, their love,
They will feel how pure the motive
That has led them to reprove.

The anniversaries at the Bowery Mission were always notable occasions and every convert made a special effort to be present, many of them coming from quite a distance. I was present and made a short address at sixteen of these gatherings; and on each occasion also wrote a hymn. Victor H. Benke, for so many years their organist, was one of my best friends; and he composed the music to a number of my hymns. Mrs. Bird, "my singing bird," as I call her, and the Rev. Mr. Hallimond, at present in charge of the Bowery Mission, with many other faithful souls, have carried forward the work so nobly commenced more than thirty years ago.

Jerry McAuley, for many years, was one of the most widely known men in New York. It was in his own mission in Water Street that I first met him; but the story of his life, how he had been a thief, a drunkard and a thoroughly desperate man, was familiar to me, and I was deeply interested in him because of the work of grace wrought at his conversion. As a speaker he used simple language, but his manner was so impressive that all men were drawn toward him. He and his faithful wife toiled and planned and sacrificed to give the old Water Street Mission a start. Not long after my first visit with them they were instrumental in founding the Cremorne Mission on West Thirty-second Street; and there I believe I was introduced to Mrs. E. M. Whittemore, the founder of the Door of Hope for unprotected girls.

I was at once wonderfully impressed by the earnestness of this remarkable lady; and I lost no occasion to inquire concerning her work. One of the incidents that she related was regarding a visit to Boston. She was asked to speak at a parlor meeting, and was obliged to decline; but a few days before the time of the gathering she felt prompted to make an extra effort to attend. She had recently received a letter directed to "Mrs. Whittemore, United States of America"; and this was found to have been written by a poor heartbroken father in Ireland in behalf of his wandering daughter whom he supposed to be somewhere in America.

With the subject of the letter still on her mind, Mrs. Whittemore spoke at the meeting in Boston. The house proved to be too small for the audience that collected; and so they adjourned to a neighboring church. While she was speaking she noticed two girls standing near the door; and when the meeting was concluded they were introduced to her, and she asked a few questions as to their circumstances. Little by little, it dawned on her that one of them was the girl referred to in the letter she had received from Ireland; and she gave her the letter her father had written. The poor unfortunate girl nearly fainted when she recognized the handwriting; and as a result of her providential meeting with Mrs. Whittemore, she was also reconciled to the young man who had deserted her. For, in the meanwhile, he too, had been converted and had been brought to the notice of Mrs. Whittemore; who was thus enabled to be the means of helping them to a happy ending of their romance and they returned to their home in Ireland.

It has been my good fortune to know both of the Hadley brothers, who have been such mighty forces for good in the missions of New York. Col. Henry Hadley I met many years before his conversion, which occurred at the Jerry McAuley Mission. When I first knew him he was a skeptic and was in many ways hostile to the Christian cause, although he was always very kind to everyone. At that time he was a successful lawyer and the editor of a prominent New York paper. I became acquainted with him through a request to write some verses relative to an incident that had recently attracted considerable attention from the public press. As Colonel Hadley gave it to me it was something as follows: A woman had been convicted by one of our city judges and sent to jail. The next morning her little boy came to the judge's room and stood in silence before the magistrate.

"Well, what can I do for you?" curiously asked the judge.

"Please, sir, let my mother go," answered the little fellow.

"Who is your mother?" inquired the judge.

"She came here yesterday," said the boy; and gave her name.

"Oh," replied the magistrate, "I cannot let that woman go." But the boy pleaded.

"She is so good to me. She buys my clothes and shoes, and sends me to school; and goes without things herself for me; and—please sir—what am I going to do without her?"

Such argument had more weight than the law. It was irresistible, and the stern judge for once quickly yielded. Brushing the tears from his eyes he called for the prisoner to be brought. Then he gave her a sharp reprimand and let her go home with the boy. The woman threw her arms around her little defender saying, "My boy, your mother will never disgrace you again."

This was the story that Colonel Henry H. Hadley wished me to put into verse. The story remains, but my poem has been forgotten.

Then Colonel Hadley asked me to write once in every two weeks for his paper.

Once he called for some verses asking me to urge men not to drink intoxicants during business hours; and then a poem pleading with them not to drink for twenty-four hours, as an experiment to see if they could quit the habit; and finally he asked for a piece imploring them not to drink at all. The first two of my poems were condemned by some and praised by others. A few, who believed in taking a whole loaf or no bread at all said that I was openly aiding the cause of intemperance by advising men to do anything short of abstaining at once and forever. But I had confidence enough in Colonel Hadley to trust him not to use these poems in any way which the best citizens might disapprove. Colonel Hadley himself was by no means an abstainer then; but he was trying hard to break the fetters that bound him.

He was a candid man, but, although he had original ideas concerning religion, he never tried to force his views on others. We sometimes disagreed; then he would generally say, "You are all right; perhaps I shall see it as you do some day." And that glad occasion did indeed finally come through the prayers and efforts of his brother, S. H. Hadley, who had been saved at the Cremorne Mission.

For months prior to Colonel Hadley's conversion I did not see him; yet heard from time to time that he was not holding out as well as he wished against evil habits. Later there came a vague rumor that he had started over again. But this news seemed too good to be at once believed, so I waited until I should hear from him direct; for I knew if the report were true he would come to me, sooner or later, and relate all the circumstances that led him to become a Christian. One evening, almost three months later, I heard a ring at the door about nine o'clock, and someone asking, "Is Fanny Crosby up?" I knew his voice and was convinced that he had come to tell me the glad news of his conversion.

"I have something to tell her," he said, "I have found the Lord." When I reached the door I exclaimed,

"Bless you, Colonel Hadley, come right upstairs and tell me all about it." When I asked why he had not called before he said,

"Oh, I wanted to be sure that I would hold out." Col. Henry Hadley became a great power for God; and during the seventeen years of his Christian life he founded sixty missions, many of which became permanent. I was acquainted with his brother, the late Samuel H. Hadley, for twenty-five years; and it was always a rare pleasure to go down to the old Water Street Mission and see the wonderful work that was being done there for the spread of the Master's kingdom; but the two brothers have now clasped their hands in glory.

My work among the missions of New York has been largely supplemented, during the last thirty years, by that among the Young Men's Christian Associations in various cities. Richard C. Morse, a prince among workers, was known to me as early as 1868; and one morning—I think it was in 1871—he came to my home before I had eaten my breakfast, and asked,

"What are you going to do today?"

I replied that I had no particular plans and was entirely at his service, if I could do any good. He then told me the sad story of a poor drunkard who had attempted to commit suicide. Mr. Morse had taken the unfortunate man to his own room; had given him something to eat; and, as he appeared to be more comfortable had now come to me to see what we together could do for his conversion. The man was finally redeemed and afterwards became a minister of the gospel.

That was really my first work among men. It antedates the commencement of my labors among missions by three or four years; and it was not until 1880 that I conducted frequent services for the railroad branches of the Christian Association. As I was entering a surface car one afternoon I chanced to step on the conductor's foot; and I cried,

"O, conductor, I know that I have hurt you, but I did not intend to. Will you please forgive me?" He replied,

"You didn't hurt me at all; and if you had you made up for it by speaking a kind word." I believe it was his remark that turned my attention toward the work among railroad men; and it was not long after this that an opportunity came for its commence-

Before an audience

ment. Before the month had passed I was invited to the home of my friend William Rock, who was superintendent of a surface car line in New York. He was in the habit of gathering a few Christian men together on each Sabbath morning to hold a prayer service for the railway employees. Only a few came at first, but finally the little room in the car station was filled with railroad "boys." Although this was not a permanent organization, Mr. Rock's little company formed one of the first associations of railroad men in active Christian work.

The following year I met three members of the Railroad Branch of the Y.M.C.A., which had recently been organized at Hoboken. They were Tom Keenan, Jerry George, and James Berwick and these three men, together with Benjamin Locke, formed a quartet of earnest workers in whom I have since been interested. A week after our meeting—which occurred in New York at my photographer's—they invited me to visit the association at Hoboken. There I met Mr. J. L. B. Sunderlin, then secretary in that city; and now at Albany; and from that date at least twice each year we have held a very pleasant reunion.

Since 1882 I have addressed the men of the Christian Association in various towns and cities; and they have given me such a warm place in their affections that I have been obliged to adopt five or six hundred of them throughout the Eastern States. They, however, in turn have adopted me; and the Hoboken Branch some years ago gave me a beautiful little badge of honorary membership.

The rapid growth of the Y.M.C.A. gratifies my heart, and I am very glad to know that railway officials and other employers are coming to realize more and more that it is to their mutual advantage to encourage this noble work. In witness of the growing sentiment in favor of the Y.M.C.A. I need but refer to the increasing number of buildings that are erected yearly for the accommodation of the young men of all classes, and for their intellectual and moral improvement.

I am glad to be able to quote a stanza from a Christmas poem written for the railroad branch of the Young Men's Christian Association about ten years ago:

> How I would like to shake your hands,
>   And greet you one by one;
> But we are now too far apart,
>   And this cannot be done.
> Yet I can hope, and wish, and pray
>   That heaven's eternal joys
> May fall like dew upon your heads,
>   My noble railroad boys.

19

Events of Recent Years

My dear mother, who was so many years a comfort to me, passed peacefully from this world to that brighter home above, September 2, 1890. She had lived to attain the grand old age of ninety-one years; and had always enjoyed good health until a short time before her death. Her last days were calm and beautiful, a blessing to all who knew her. A short time after her death, as a tribute of my devotion to her, I composed the following poem:

Her voyage of life is ended,
  Her anchor firmly cast,
Her bark that many a storm has braved
  Is safe in port at last.
Surrounded by her treasured ones,
  Our mother passed away
Beneath the golden sunset
  Of summer's brightest day.

She waited for the summons
That called her to depart,
And heard the voice of Jesus
    Like music in her heart.
Not hopeless in our sorrow
    We lay her down to sleep,
Where he, our Lord and Savior,
    A hallowed watch will keep.

We loved our tender mother
    Far more than words can tell,
And while with deep emotion
    We breathe our fond farewell,
We know her tranquil spirit
    Has reached the longed-for shore,
And now with joy is greeting
    The loved ones gone before.

Oh, mother, we are coming;
    The time will not be long
Till we shall clasp thy hand again,
    And join the blessed song.
The sheaf of wheat is garnered,
    The sickle's work is done,
And everlasting glory
    Through Christ her soul has won.

Besides often making addresses before various
religious bodies, such as the Young Men's Christian
Associations, Sabbath schools and churches of many
creeds, during the last twenty years, I have been led
to write some of my most abiding hymns: "Jesus Is
Calling," "My Savior First of All," "Blessed Day,"
"Resting by the River," "Never Say Good-Bye," "He
Hideth My Soul," "Meet Me There," "Come with

Rejoicing," "Safe in the Glory Land," and "Yes, There Is Pardon for You." "How many hymns have you written?" is a question I often hear. The exact number has never been recorded but the Biglow and Main Company inform me that I have written five thousand five hundred for them alone; and I may have composed half as many more for several authors of music. None of the infirmities incident to old age have touched me as yet; and my active labors still continue amid the many kind friends whom God has sent to enrich this early life. Among these are I. Allan Sankey, who has set the notes to many of my hymns, Hubert P. Main, Sidney A. Saunders, and George Leonard, all of whom are, or have been, associated with the Biglow and Main Company of New York.

This firm in 1897 issued a volume of my poems, entitled "Bells at Evening and Other Verses," and containing one hundred twenty-four pages. The initial poem, which gave the title to the book, was inspired by a little reminiscence of the lovely village of Ledyard, New York, where I visited more than fifty years ago; and the incident narrated is partly true and partly imaginative.

The city of Bridgeport has always had peculiar attractions for me, not only because it has long been the home of most of those who are near my heart by ties of blood, but because also of the delightful acquaintance of many of her generous citizens. Prior to 1900, therefore, my sisters had urged me, for some years, to give up my residence in New York; and thus to consider this city my

permanent home. To this end they were heartily
seconded by my publishers, who wished to relieve
me, as much as possible, after a busy life, from the
care and anxiety to which my life as a hymn writer
necessarily was subjected; and principally to place
me under the immediate care of those who were
ready and willing to do everything in their power to
render me the happiest mortal in the world. But I
did not accede to their request until, in 1900, through
a serious illness, the good Lord overruled my objec-
tion to what seemed like a partial retirement from
active labors; and so in May of that year I bade
farewell to my many friends in New York, assuring
them that I should visit them frequently, as I believed in the enjoyment of perfect health. This has
indeed been true; since the fresh and invigorating
air did what it had done for me a number of times
before, when I came to Bridgeport on visits to my
mother. And I need not say that here I found a most
cordial welcome from those whom I had loved so
long and well. Besides my beloved sisters, Mrs. Julia
M. Athington and Mrs. Carrie W. Rider, Mrs.
Athington has a daughter, Mrs. Leschon; and I had
one brother, William, who died in 1880, leaving
three children, Laura Frances, now Mrs. William
Tait; Florence, now Mrs. Henry D. Booth; and Albert
Morris, who married Miss Clara Hope; all of whom,
with their children, live near me, and serve to make
my life like a stream without a ripple upon its
silver waters, or a sky without a cloud to dim the
golden sunlight. Besides I have cousins in Hartford,
Bridgeport, Savannah, Georgia, and New York City.

Each summer for seven years I have been making a delightful pilgrimage to the beautiful lake region of New York; and to the Chautauqua Assembly on the shores of Tully Lake. Here I have found, close to nature's heart, one of the best things that earth has to offer any mortal; and that is the immortal friendship of kindred spirits. There I have delivered annually a poem before the Chautauqua Round Table, over which Mrs. Elizabeth Snyder Roberts so genially presides, and with Mr. and Mrs. D. H. Cook, makes my visits one round of happy experiences. On the shores of Tully Lake I also renewed my friendship with Dr. Israel Parsons and Miss Eliza E. Hewitt; and with them have passed many happy hours in delightful conversation. Miss Hewitt, by her modest efforts, wins the affectionate regard of all who come to know her; and some of her hymns, I am sure, like "There's Sunshine in My Soul," "Will There Be Any Stars in My Crown?" "Never Alone," "Jesus Is Passing By," and many others equally familiar, will never die. Mr. Will A. Post, who writes a great many sweet melodies, is also a frequent visitor in our sylvan home; and there each summer we meet our dear friends, Mrs. Harriett Blair Bristol, Mrs. Nellie R. Willis and Miss Elizabeth Corey, besides others with whom I delight to hold sweet communion.

It was also at Assembly Park that I first became acquainted, through his own poems, with that modest friend and companion who has, from the beginning, aided me generously and unselfishly, in the writing of this book; but neither of us dreamed at the first meeting that the stream of friendship, touching the lives of both, would flow onward so pleasantly without a ripple to disturb the bosom of its placid waters.

Next to good bandits I have been deeply interested in the Indians; and you may be sure that I was highly delighted, as well as honored, when Albert Cusick, formerly chief of the Six Nations, told me that he would adopt me into the Eel Clan of the Onondagas. The rite of adoption was performed in the summer of 1904; but you need have no fear of me, for the hatchet has been buried these many years.

Being now an Indian myself, it will not be amiss to tell an Indian legend, which has descended from generation to generation among the Onondagas from time immemorial; and it concerns the brave warrior Hiawatha, that young chief of the Onondagas, whose heroic deeds have been so often mentioned in story and in song.

For many moons, the legend tells us, Hiawatha desired to unite the tribes of Central New York into one federation. So he started on a journey to smoke the pipe of peace with the Mohawks; and arriving at the shore of Tully Lake he stopped to gaze on the shining waters as they caught the noonday sun. Suddenly a flock of birds flew over the lake to the northward; and the waters followed them, but Hiawatha could not tell whither the birds or water went. Looking down he saw a quantity of shells; and yet the mystery was not solved. But he gathered some of them, and continued his journey until he arrived at the hunting grounds of the Mohawks. The chief and his people were much delighted to see Hiawatha; his collection of shells attracted much attention. They were willing to exchange blankets and corn for some of the bright trinkets; and, thus, according to the legend of the Onondagas, began the use of shells for Indian money.

As I go about the country I often meet former associates and not a few friends with whom I review the events of the past. My old home at the New York Institution is still dear to me, although there are few left there to welcome me when I enter its sacred halls. Since the death of Annie Sheridan, a few months ago, there are only two, Hannah Rodney and Alice Hatchman, left there of all those who were my pupils. They were kind and affectionate to me; and although the roses of youth have faded and we are walking along the vale of mature years, our love is unclouded and our friendship unbroken.

There are a few other pupils living in distant cities with whom I often correspond: Ellen Teft and Susan McLean of Syracuse; and now and then I hear of others in various states.

Mr. Stephen Babcock was a teacher in the Institution for more than forty years and is remembered also by me as one of my pupils, and still two other friendships have come down to me as rich legacies from the past: Mr. William B. Wait, who has served as superintendent of the Institution since 1864; and during the last forty years of very faithful and efficient service has endeared himself to both pupils and teachers; and Mr. Harvey Fuller, who has been one of my most intimate friends and whose books have been an inspiration to me. Within a day or two I have received a copy of his last book of poems entitled "Hidden Beauties" and have heard it read with great interest.

I look back with tender emotions and gratitude to the many friends and acquaintances who joined to make the occasion of my eighty-fifth birthday, March 24, 1905, most delightful. Not only America but England and the far-off lands of India and Tasmania were lavish in their congratulations; and in the fullness of my heart I exclaimed, "Surely 'the lines are fallen to me in pleasant places; yea I have a goodly heritage.'" A part of my birthday—as has been my custom for over twenty years—was spent with the Biglow and Main Company in New York; and in the evening the good people of Bridgeport united in giving me a reception at the First Methodist Church, which was followed on the next Sunday evening by an address and impromptu reception at the First Baptist Church. This latter church gave me as a birthday gift a dollar for each year of my life.

A friend of mine, who has been quite interested in my book, has asked me to allow her permission to give the following pen-picture of my personal appearance on the evening of my birthday at the reception: "Miss Crosby wore a most becoming dress of brocaded satin, ashes of roses I believe they call the color, with a white chiffon front and a narrow piping on each side of the vest of pink and black velvet, which was very dainty and pretty. As she walked up the aisle, it was suggested that the audience wave their handkerchiefs; and the effect thus produced was as if a white cloud of doves was fluttering over the heads of all, suggesting to those who know Miss Crosby the peace and good will she sheds abroad upon our hearts by her life of song and of good cheer." The dress above described was also a birthday gift, presented to me by my dear friends, Mr. and Mrs. R. B. Currier.

Certain rumors have been circulated among some of the good people who do not know me to the effect that my health is fast declining. About fifteen years ago there was a gentleman in New York, who, hearing that I was dead, took the occasion to preach a funeral sermon; at another time my publishers received a telegram, while I was in the act of dictating a hymn that I had just written, asking at what hour Fanny Crosby passed away; and at still another time a great New York paper, while I was sitting at home in perfect health, published the intelligence that my death was momentarily expected—but none of these things moved me. Nor do I myself believe any of the recent reports as to the declining state of my health; where they originated I do not care. To the good Lord be the praise that they are not true; and I patiently await the time when He himself shall come to write my obituary in the Book of Life, until when I hope to continue to labor with all the energy that I can command.

Not long ago, while I was visiting in Metuchen, New Jersey, a friend came to me and said, "I think we have your old organ at our church." She spoke of a favorite instrument upon which I used to play at the Institution; but at first I could not believe that it was really in existence, for I had understood that it had been destroyed many years ago. They led me to it and said I might finger the beloved keys again, as I had done so many times. It was a rare opportunity, and I confess that I shed tears of joy, yet a very sweet feeling took possession of me as I played some of the old melodies that we loved and sang more than sixty years ago. I fancied that time had turned backward and had borne me to those halls again, where I could hear the familiar voices of our pupils singing the classic melodies. There was Mr. Reiff speaking kind words to his scholars; there was our quartet singing before Henry Clay and General Scott; there was Jenny Lind again pouring forth her soul in some Swedish or American patriotic air; and Ole Bull again held us spellbound by the touching melodies of his beloved violin; and I thanked the good Father for permitting me to enjoy that happy hour which was indeed the earnest of a happy life.

Most of the beloved voices of our Institution chorus are now blending with the grand anthem of the choir invisible in the great tuneful city. But to me they are not hushed forevermore, because I sometimes fancy that I can hear the sweet, low notes of the celestial melodies. Meanwhile the music of the voices around me here upon this beautiful earth is just as cheerful and inspiring as that I heard in years gone by. Thus life becomes one grand choral song, sweetest at its close; and the tender acts of kindness, strewn all along the way, are the perennial flowers that I have been transplanting and gleaning in the garden of memory for more than eighty summers.

20

Incidents of Hymns

The most enduring hymns are born in the silences of the soul, and nothing must be allowed to intrude while they are being framed into language. Some of the sweetest melodies of the heart never see the light of the printed page. Sometimes the song without words has a deeper meaning than the more elaborate combinations of words and music. But in the majority of instances these two must be joined in marriage; and unless they are mutually complementary the resulting hymn will not please. The mere fitting of words to a melody is by no means all that is necessary; it must be so well done as to have the effect of having been written especially for that melody. The poet, therefore, must put into metrical form his thoughts, aspirations and emotions, in such a manner that the composer of the music may readily grasp the spirit of the poem and compose notes that will perfect the expression of the poet's meaning. And a similar harmony of thought must exist between the composer of the melody and the poet when the music is written first.

That some of my hymns have been dictated by the blessed Holy Spirit I have no doubt; and that others have been the result of deep meditation I know to be true; but that the poet has any right to claim special merit for himself is certainly presumptuous. I have sometimes felt that there was a deep and clear well of inspiration from which one may draw the sparkling draughts that are so essential to good poetry. At times the burden of inspiration is so heavy that the author himself cannot find words beautiful enough, or thoughts deep enough, for its expression.

Most of my poems have been written during the long night watches, when the distractions of the day could not interfere with the rapid flow of thought. It has been my custom to hold a little book in my hand; and somehow or other the words seem to come more promptly when I am so engaged. I can also remember more accurately when the little volume is in my grasp. Many people, noting this peculiar custom, have asked some queer questions about it; and not a few fancy that I may indeed be able to see what is printed there. Sometimes a hymn comes to me by stanzas and needs only to be written down, but I never have any portion of a poem committed to paper until the entire poem is composed; then there is often much pruning and revising necessary before it is really finished. Some poems, it is true, come as a complete whole, and need no

revision—indeed the best seem to come that way—
but the great majority do not. "Safe in the Arms of
Jesus" was composed and written in less than thirty
minutes; but I have often spent three or four hours
on half as many lines, and then cast them aside as
worthless.

In composing hymn-poems there are several ways
of working. Often subjects are given to me to which
melodies must be adapted. At other times the melody is played for me and I think of various subjects
appropriate to the music. In a successful song words
and music must harmonize, not only in number of
syllables, but in subject matter and especially ac-
cent. In nine cases out of ten the success of a hymn
depends directly upon these qualities. Thus, melodies tell their own tale, and it is the purpose of the
poet to interpret this musical story into language.
Not infrequently a composer asks, "What does that
melody say to you?" And if it says nothing to you
the probability is that your words will not agree
with the music when an attempt is made to join
them. "Blessed Assurance" was written to a melody
composed by my friend, Mrs. Joseph F. Knapp; she
played it over once or twice on the piano and then
asked me what it is said to me. I replied,

> Blessed assurance, Jesus is mine,
> O what a foretaste of glory divine!
> Heir of salvation, purchase of God,
> Born of his spirit, washed in his blood:
> This is my story, this is my song,
> Praising my Savior all the day long.

The hymn thus written seemed to express the experience of both Mrs. Knapp and myself.

Generally, when a melody is given, I choose my own subject. Sometimes the melody suggests the subject at once; if it does not I lay it aside until another time. Sometimes the words to the melody come to me faster than I can remember them. One evening, for instance, Mr. Sankey played a sweet air. I excused myself and went to my room to compose the words to "O My Redeemer." In this way I wrote "I Am Thine, O Lord" to a melody written by Mr. Doane; and "When My Life Work Is Ended" to one written by Mr. Sweney.

Among the great number of hymns that I have written—eight thousand perhaps—it is not always possible for me to remember even the best of them. For this reason I have made laughable mistakes. One morning, for example, at Northfield the audience sang "Hide Me, O My Savior, Hide Me." But I did not recognize this hymn as my own production; and therefore I may be pardoned for saying that I was much pleased with it. Turning to Mr. Sankey, I asked, "Where did you get that piece?" He paid no particular attention to my question, for he supposed I was merely joking; and at that moment the bell called us to dinner—so both of us forgot about the hymn. But it was again used at the afternoon service; and then I was determined to know who wrote it.

"Mr. Sankey," I said, "Now you must tell me who is the author of 'Hide Me, O My Savior.'"

"Really," he replied, "don't you recall who wrote that hymn? You ought to remember, for you are the guilty one."

A large number of my hymns have gone out into the world bearing noms-de-plume; and hundreds are yet to be set to notes; but enough have already been published to make me wish to avoid so many credits for authorship; hence the long list of pseudonyms that I have adopted. According to Mr. Hubert P. Main, who collected them all, this list reached almost the hundred mark; many of the names, however, were used once or twice, or at most only for a single book; and a large number of initials have been used, especially in early collections. Some of the most frequently used pen-names are James Apple, Mrs. A. E. Andrews, Rose Atherton, James Black, Henrietta E. Blair, Florence Booth, Charles Bruce, Robert Bruce, Leah Carlton, Lyman Cuyler, Ella Dale, Lizzie Edwards, James Eliott, Grace J. Frances, Rian J. Dykes, Victoria Frances, Jennie Garnet, Jenie Glen, Frank Gould, Mrs. Kate Grinley, Ruth Harmon, Frances Hope, Martha J. Lankton, W. Robert Lindsay, Sally Martin, Sam Martin, Maud Marion, Alice Montieth, Sally Smith, Sam Smith, Victoria Stewart, Victoria Sterling, Rian J. Sterling, Julia Sterling and Mrs. C. M. Wilson.

The hymn "O Child of God, Wait Patiently" came into being at Northfield. Mr. Sankey played a pretty air and said,

"Why not write a poem for this tonight?" But the

spirit of poetry was not with me that evening; and so I replied,

"No, I cannot at present; for I have few ideas and they are not poetic." The following morning Mr. and Mrs. Sankey were going for a drive, and they expected that I would go with them; but, to their astonishment, I said,

"Please excuse me today; as I have something else I wish to do." A few minutes after they left a number of students came in; and we had a very pleasant chat. Something that one of them said touched my heart; and after they went away I sat down at the piano; played Mr. Sankey's melody once or twice; and then the words of the hymn came in regular order as they now stand:

> O child of God, wait patiently
>   When dark thy path may be,
> And let thy faith lean trustingly
>   On Him who cares for thee;
> And though the clouds hang drearily
>   Upon the brow of night;
> Yet in the morning joy will come,
>   And fill thy soul with light.

While the great majority of my hymns seemed to be the result of some passing mood, or of some deep, though intangible feeling, whose expression demanded the language of poetry, quite a number were called into being in response to a definite event in my own life. "Hold Thou My Hand," for which Hubert P. Main wrote the music, belongs to this class. For a number of days before I wrote this hymn, all had seemed dark to me. That was indeed an unusual experience, for I have always been most cheerful; and so in my human weakness I cried in prayer, "Dear Lord, hold thou my hand." Almost at once the sweet peace that comes of perfect assurance returned to my heart, and my gratitude for this evidence of answered prayer sang itself in the lines of the hymn,

> Hold thou my hand, so weak I am and helpless,
> I dare not take one step without thy aid;
> Hold thou my hand, for then, O loving Savior
> No dread of ill shall make my soul afraid.

After the death of the great Charles Spurgeon his wife wrote for a copy of this poem and said she had found comfort from hearing it sung.

Once while on a visit to William J. Kirkpatrick some of us were talking of how soon we grow weary of earthly pleasures, however bright they may be.

"Well," remarked the professor, "we are never weary of the grand old song."

"No," I replied, "but what comes next?" He hesitated and I said, "Why, glory to God, hallelujah." Mr. Kirkpatrick sang an appropriate melody and I wrote the hymn,

> We are never, never weary of the grand old song,
> Glory to God, hallelujah!

We can sing it in the Spirit as we march along,
  Glory to God, hallelujah!

Besides this I have written hundreds of hymns for
Mr. Kirkpatrick, many of which have been very
popular, and are still being sung in all quarters of
the Christian world. One day he played a beautiful
melody and said, "Now let us have a regular shouting
Methodist hymn," and I composed the hymn "I'm
So Glad," the chorus of which is,

I'm so glad, I'm so glad,
I'm so glad that Jesus came,
He came to save me.

"Speed Away, Speed Away, on your Mission of
Light" was written after hearing the beautiful Indian
melody which Mr. Sankey arranged for my words.
The original Indian poem told the story of a young
maiden who died leaving her father to mourn her
untimely loss, and how he was comforted by a
message brought him by a bird she had sent from
the happy hunting grounds. This melody seemed so
beautiful that we thought it ought to have hymn-
like words and "Speed Away" was the outcome of
this feeling. I wrote it hoping that it might inspire
someone to go into the mission fields across the
sea.

One day Mr. Doane played the air to "We Shall
Reach the Summer Land," and we thought it best to

wait for an appropriate subject. A few days later a telegram came announcing the death of a friend; and I wrote a hymn to his music for the bereaved family. "No Sorrow There" was also written under similar circumstances. "God Leadeth" was inspired by the sympathy I felt with a friend in his struggles, and a number of hymns have been written after conversing with friends concerning various phases of Christian experience. "Press Toward the Mark" was inspired by a watchnight address by Dr. Theodore L. Cuyler and the music was composed by Miss Upham.

"Jesus, My All" was written as early as 1866. Someone was singing the air to the old Scotch song "Robin Adair," and I remarked how beautiful it was. Henry Brown said, "I challenge you to write a hymn to that melody." I immediately wrote the words following,

> Lord, at thy mercy-seat,
>   Humbly I fall,
> Pleading thy promise sweet,
>   Lord, hear my call;
> Now let thy work begin,
>   Oh, make me pure within,
> Cleanse me from every sin,
>   Jesus, my all.

Another of the hymns written during Mr. Bradbury's life is, "Good Night Until We Meet in the Morning." One afternoon a little party of us, including Philip Phillips, William B. Bradbury, Sylvester Main, Harry Brown and myself, were talking about various things, and when we came to separate Mr. Phillips said,

"Good night until we meet in the morning."

The idea caught my fancy at once; and I said to Mr. Bradbury,

"If I write a hymn for that subject, will you compose the music?" He said that he would; and the words were written that same evening. Other hymns written before 1868 are "The Prodigal's Return," "Let the Good Angels Come In," "Lord, Abide with Me," "Welcome Hour of Prayer" and "Our Loved Ones Gone Before."

On April 30, 1868, Dr. W. H. Doane came into my house, and said,

"I have exactly forty minutes before my train leaves for Cincinnati. Here is a melody. Can you write words for it?" I replied that I would see what I could do. Then followed a space of twenty minutes during which I was wholly unconscious of all else except the work I was doing. At the end of that time I recited the words to "Safe in the Arms of Jesus." Mr. Doane copied them, and had time to catch his train.

There are a great many beautiful stories connected with this hymn. Ira D. Sankey related a conversation with a simple Scotch woman who came to him after a great meeting.

"I want to thank you for writing 'Safe in the Arms of Jesus,'" she said.

"My daughter was very fond of it and sang it as she passed to the life beyond."

"But," replied the evangelist, "I did not write the hymn. Fanny Crosby wrote the words and W. H. Doane the music. Sit down, my good woman, and I will tell you about it." A look of disappointment passed over the dear woman's face; but as she listened to Mr. Sankey's story her countenance again lighted up and she said,

"When ye gang back to America tell Fanny Crosby that an auld Scots woman sends her blessing and her love."

The late Dr. John Hall used to tell a touching story of "Safe in the Arms of Jesus." He went to see the little daughter of one of his congregation; and her father came downstairs in tears.

"My dear friend," asked the clergyman, "what is the trouble? Has the little girl gone home?"

"No," replied the father, "but she has asked me to do something that I cannot do; anything that wealth might buy she may have, but I cannot sing 'Safe in the Arms of Jesus'; for I never sang a note in my life."

"Oh," said Dr. Hall, "I will go up and sing it for her." When he reached the last two lines of the hymn

> Wait till I see the morning
> Break on the golden shore.

the spirit of the child passed to that land where all shall sing the melodies of Zion.

Another incident of the singing of "Safe in the Arms of Jesus" was related by a sea captain, who was in the habit of holding services on board his vessel. From Sabbath to Sabbath he noticed that there was a certain man who did not unite with the others when they sang that hymn. At last he approached the sailor and inquired if he did not enjoy the meetings.

"Oh, yes," the latter replied, "but I am not 'safe in the arms of Jesus'; and I cannot sing that hymn." The captain prayed with him, and as a direct result of the interview, ere the next Sabbath, the sailor was singing the piece with the rest.

On one occasion as Mr. Doane and I were traveling from Cincinnati to New York he composed a melody which he whistled to me, and suggested that I compose the words to accompany it. I told him I would, and in a short time I wrote the hymn beginning,

Jesus, I love thee, thou art to me
Dearer than mortal ever can be.

This hymn was published in a book called "The Diadem" and copied into an English song collection. A few years later Mr. Doane received a letter from England, written at the request of a dying woman by her pastor. She had been brought under conviction by the singing of our hymn; had given herself to the Lord; and before her death had been the means of leading over twenty souls into the light. Some years after this Mr. Doane attended a large meeting at Vernon, Ohio; and after the service a man came to him and asked,

"Do you remember receiving a letter from a gentleman in England concerning a lady's conversion after hearing 'Jesus, I Love Thee'? Well, I am the one who wrote the letter." Mr. Doane told me the meeting seemed providential.

Some years after the writing of "Jesus, I Love Thee" Mr. Stebbins came to me and said,

"I think I have something both of us will enjoy. I have a melody here, and would like to have you write the words for it while we are together." He played it over for me and I was pleased with the tune and wrote "They Tell Us of a Land So Fair." Mr. Stebbins also wrote the music to "Jesus Is Calling," "No Sorrow There," "The Day Star Hath Risen," "O Sing of My Redeemer," and many others.

"Victory Through Grace" was written under the following circumstances: Mr. Sweney sent me the title and asked me to write a sort of a battle piece. A day or two later he came to see me. I told him I had already begun the hymn; and repeated as much as I had finished. "Go on," he said, "that is right; we'll have our battle song." The remainder of the hymn was written while he was at my house. Mr. Sweney also wrote the music to "Only a Beam of Sunshine," "The Savior Precious" and "Sing On," and scores of others.

It was a cold, rainy day, and everything had gone wrong with me during the morning. I realized that the fault was mine; but that did not help the matter. About noon the sky began to be clear; and a friend standing near me said, "There is only a beam of sunshine, but, oh, it is warm and bright"; and, on the impulse of the moment, I wrote the hymn,

Only a beam of sunshine, but, oh, it was warm and bright,
The heart of a weary traveler was cheered by its welcome light.

"Now Just a Word for Jesus" was written with the idea of influencing people at prayer meetings to give their testimonies and to give them promptly. One day someone was talking about wealth; and he said, "If I had wealth I would be able to do just what I wish to do; and I would be able to make an appearance in the world." I replied, "Take the world, but give me Jesus." This remark led me to write the hymn having that title.

On one occasion Mr. Kirkpatrick had been at my home; and as he was going away I said,

"Oh, dear, it's nothing but meeting and parting in this world, is it?" He replied,

"Well, I will not say as Bliss did 'meet me at the fountain,' but I will say, 'where the tree of life is blooming, meet me there.'" Not long afterward I wrote the hymn entitled "Meet Me There."

"I Am Satisfied" was written during the summer of 1902 while I was visiting Dr. William H. Doane.

The "blind singer" at home

One morning I received a telegram announcing the death of a very dear friend; and it occurred to me that under the circumstances it would be well for me to occupy my mind by writing as many hymns as I could. I accordingly secluded myself where I could hear the music of Old Ocean, and wrote "I Am Satisfied."

Mr. Sylvester Main was a little depressed one day, and I said that if we were always at peace with God these trials would not annoy us as they do now.

"No," he replied, "and I very often have to exclaim, 'Lord, abide with me'"; and his remark inspired me to write the hymn bearing this title.

"Valley of Eden, Beyond the Sea" is one of my hymns of which I have erred concerning the authorship. On one occasion I heard a lady singing it, and I rushed downstairs, exclaiming,

"Where did you get that beautiful melody and words?"

"Well," she replied, "Mr. Kirkpatrick wrote the melody."

"But," I said, "who wrote those words?" She replied, "Someone who is in the habit of writing for him." Even then I did not recognize my own words; and she finally said that she would sing the hymn once more, which she did; and to my embarrassment I remembered writing it.

Dr. Lowry gave me the subject to "the bright forever" and I tried for two days to write the hymn. Then all at once, almost in a twinkling, the words came stanza by stanza as fast as I could memorize them. Hubert P. Main wrote the music, which has done so much to popularize the hymn. He also wrote the notes for "Hold Thou My Hand" (in 1874) "Blessed Homeland," "Yes, There Is Pardon for You," and other hymns.

"Blessed Assurance" was written in 1873. The music was composed by Mrs. Joseph F. Knapp, who became known to me as early as 1868, and who has also written the notes to several hymns of mine, including "Nearer The Cross," and "Open the Gates of the Temple." An English religious weekly gives the following account of how soldiers use "God Be With You" and "Blessed Assurance" for passwords. When one member of the Soldiers' Christian Association meets a comrade he says "494" which is the number of "God Be With You Till We Meet Again" in "Sacred Songs and Solos"; the latter replies "6 farther on," that is 500, which is the number of "Blessed Assurance." Of this custom the secretary of the Association writes, "These hymns are constantly being used by our members as greeting and response; and I do not think any member of the Soldiers' Christian Association ever writes without putting them somewhere on the letter or envelope. I have had dozens of letters from South Africa alone; and in my visits to garrisons and soldiers' homes no meeting is considered closed until 'God Be With You' has been sung."

In one of Mr. Sankey's meetings a man came forward and requested that someone offer a prayer for him. He appeared to be deeply distressed in spirit; and when they said that he might come again the next night, he cried earnestly,

"No, it must be settled tonight; for tomorrow may be too late." They listened to his appeal, and before he left the church he felt that he was saved. The next day there was an explosion in the mine where he worked, and he was among the slain. This story was related to me by Mr. Sankey and I wrote the hymn "Shall I Be Saved Tonight?"

"Saw Ye Not the Promised Day?" a missionary hymn, to which William F. Sherwin wrote the music, was inspired by a remark that the day of the Lord was coming.

"Pass Me Not, O Gentle Savior" (1868) was written not long after the hymn "More Like Jesus," the incident relating to which has already been told. A number of stories have been called forth by the singing of that hymn; and perhaps the best of these is the following: In a Western state lived an old man who was in the habit of going fishing on Sunday afternoons. Near the pond was a small school house in which was held a Sabbath school. Frequently they used to sing "Pass Me Not" during the afternoon service; and for some reason, he knew not why, the old man could not forget that melody. One day he could resist no longer; he threw down his fishing rod, and went up to the school house. They invited him into the Sunday school, but he said,

"No, I cannot go in today; for I am not dressed well enough." He finally promised to enter on the condition that the children should sing "Pass Me Not, O Gentle Savior." For more than fifty years he had not darkened the church door; but the old

memories began to come back again; and he could
not resist their appeal. Two years later he attended a
convention at which Dr. Doane was present, and
related the story, concluding with the words, "God
bless William H. Doane and Fanny Crosby."

"Rescue the Perishing," as I have intimated, was
written after a meeting at one of the New York
missions. Sometime after the hymn became known
I was at a service one evening and a young man told
the story of his conversion. Poor and hungry, he had
walked the streets for want of something better to
do. He heard the singing at a mission; he went in;
and before the service was concluded his heart
broke in contrition.

"I was just ready to perish," he said to me, "but
that hymn, by the grace of God saved me."

As I stood there face to face with that young man,
the audience was thrilled with the pathos of our
meeting for the first time; and tears were shed in
every part of the room.

"Only a Little Way," said a dear old lady, who had
been suffering acute pain, as she looked up into the
clear blue sky just as the sun was setting; "'tis only
a little way on to my home," and from this I wrote
the hymn bearing that title. "Jesus, Dear, I Come to
Thee," was a children's song, which I wrote, both
words and music, for the book called "Fresh Laurels," in 1867. "Lord, I Am Weary" was written
during the winter of 1867, while Mr. Bradbury was
in St. Paul, to music which he sent to Sylvester
Main. One day, before he went to Minnesota for his
health, Mr. Bradbury asked me to write a hymn to

the title, "Let the Good Angels Come In"; and when it was finished he said,

"Fanny, I am more pleased with this than I can tell you, and if there is anything I can do for you, let me know."

One afternoon Sylvester Main was humming a melody and I said to him,

"Oh, Mr. Main, that is beautiful; and if you will let me, I am going to write a hymn for it."

"Well," he said in his gentle way, "if you think it is worth it, you may do so." I composed "I Come to Thee," and it was very often sung to Mr. Main's music.

William F. Sherwin once asked me to write the words to a melody that he had composed for the May Annual, for which several Sunday schools united to sing various hymns and hold public exercises. He asked me to write a piece so smooth that the air would sing itself; and I wrote,

> Sing with a tuneful spirit,
> Sing with a cheerful lay,
> Praise to thy great creator,
> While on the pilgrim way.

Within the last five or six years I have written a number of hymns for I. Allan Sankey, among them "O Look and Live," "There's Work to Do," "Never Give Up," "Show Me Thy Way," "Bring Them In" and a "Rallying Song," for the recent Christian

Endeavor Convention, the music for which was pronounced by a friend of mine "unusually sweet and beautiful." From childhood Mr. Allan Sankey has been noted for a bright, sunny disposition; and an intense love for the arts, especially that of music, in which he has so eminently distinguished himself in later years. I used to be so fond of his playing that, on several occasions, I have neglected to write hymns, when expected to do so.

I have already told the incident concerning the first time that "Saved by Grace" was recited in public. That occurred in the summer of 1894; but the words had been written and sent to the publishers more than two years previous, although they had not yet been set to music. The hymn itself was called into being through a little incident in a sermon preached by Dr. Howard Crosby who was a distant relative and a dear friend of mine. He said that no Christian should fear death, for if each of us was faithful to the grace given us by Christ, the same grace that teaches us how to live would also teach us how to die. His remarks were afterward published in a newspaper; and they were read to me by Mr. Biglow. Not many hours after I heard them I began to write the hymn,

> Some day the silver chord will break,
>   And I as now no more shall sing,
> But, oh, the joy when I shall wake
> Within the palace of the King.

A friend sends the following story relative to "Saved by Grace." She and a companion were attending one of the auditorium meetings at Northfield; and that hymn was sung. My friend made some remark concerning her acquaintance with me; and a lady, who was sitting directly in front of her, happened to catch it. Turning around she asked eagerly,

"Did I understand you to say that you know the author of 'Saved by Grace'?" On being assured that she heard correctly, she continued,

"Will you kindly tell her what this hymn has done for me? Twelve years ago I was assailed by a great temptation at an important crisis in my life; and, although I had been a professing Christian, I was on the point of deciding for the wrong course. In this state of mind I entered a little chapel, not so much to hear the sermon as to listen to the sweet singing, and most of all to think out my own problem. Of the sermon I did not hear one word; but when the soloist began to sing, 'I Shall See Him Face to Face,' my heart melted. It seemed that God had spoken to me through the voice of that song; and I at once decided to take the right path; and ever since I have felt that the hymn saved me. I have longed to see Fanny Crosby; and if you ever meet her, please tell her the story for me."

Among the many incidents of "Saved by Grace" is one told in a small Episcopal church in Pennsylvania by a woman who had been an actress. She said that she had been indifferent to all religious influence and on a certain day was going to spend the afternoon in pleasure at one of the public parks. As she was passing along the street, unconscious of her surroundings, she was attracted by some singing; and stopped out of pure curiosity to find that an Epworth League was conducting services in the open air. They were singing "Saved by Grace" and all the tender recollections of childhood came trooping before her mental vision; and as a result of the service there that afternoon she fell on her knees and asked the forgiveness of God.

The melody to "My Savior First of All" was given me by Mr. John R. Sweney and he requested that I write something "tender and pathetic." I prayed that appropriate words might be given me for his music; and the train of thought then started finally brought me to the sweet consciousness that I will know my Savior by the print of the nails in his hand. Then I wrote,

> When my lifework is ended and I cross the swelling tide,
> When the bright and glorious morning I shall see,
> I shall know my Redeemer when I reach the other side,
> And his smile will be the first to welcome me.

The following beautiful incident was sent me not long ago. There appeared in London a man who styled himself the messiah; and for many weeks a large crowd was attracted to him. One night, however, as he was talking in one of the open squares in the city, a small band of the Salvation Army passed along singing,

> I shall know Him, I shall know Him,
>   By the print of the nails in His hand.

The great throng joined in the chorus. Finally someone pointed to the self-styled Christ and said, "Look at his hands and see if the print of the nails is there." They did as directed, but no print appeared; and they at once left off following him.

In October, 1905, while I was at Leominister, Massachusetts, I told this incident as I have just given it; and after its conclusion, a gentleman from the audience said to me,

"That story is true, every word of it; for I was there myself; and I'll never forget it."

Shortly after my mother's death in 1890 John R. Sweney requested me to send him a poem, but he did not send any subject; and so I was free to make my own selection. A title came to me, "Over the River They Call Me" and I wrote,

> Over the river they call me,
>   Friends that are dear to my heart,
> Soon I shall meet them in glory,
> Never, no never, to part.

> Over the river they call me,
>   Hark 'tis their voices I hear,
> Borne on the wings of the twilight,
>   Tenderly, softly and clear.

"Beautiful Waters of Eden" was written after I heard Prof. Adam Geibel's beautiful melody.

We were riding out one day, and Mr. Sankey said "There's sunshine on the hill, even though there are shadows in the valley," and his remark led me to write the hymn in which those words are used.

The hymn beginning

> Dark is the night, and cold the wind is blowing,
> Nearer and nearer comes the breakers' roar,

was written for Theodore E. Perkins. In one of my meetings during the autumn of 1905 a man came up to me, sang the first line of that hymn, and said, "Praise the Lord, that song was the means of my conversion, and I have been singing it for years."

> Oh, what are you going to do, brother,
>   Say what are you going to do;
> You have thought of some useful employment,
>   But what is the end in view?

was written in 1867 for Philip Phillips, who came

to me one afternoon and asked me if I could write something that would be appropriate for men of all ages, and particularly for business men.

I have already referred to my dear friend, Miss Mary E. Upham, now Mrs. R. B. Currier. For a number of years it was my good fortune to assist her as a gospel singer by contributing hymns, many of which were written after some incident. When Andrew Murray was holding evangelistic meetings in this country he was used by the Spirit to lead Mrs. Currier into deeper consecration by giving up all secular songs and using her voice only for sacred hymns. The Scripture that Dr. Murray used was the fifteenth chapter of John's Gospel; and in telling me of her experience, under the Spirit's leading I was inspired to write the hymn "Ever Abiding, Thou Keepest My Heart." This hymn and others are published in Mrs. Currier's book "O Sing Unto the Lord," for which I have used also the pseudonyms, Zemira Wallace and C. U.

"Faith" was written in response to Mrs. Currier's request to bring in all the Scripture I could bearing on that subject. "I'm Going Home to Father's House" was written and inscribed to Dr. Dixon after hearing one of his sermons about the Father's house. He had said that this world was not his home; that his home was where the Father is; and that his anchor was not cast but was lifted while he was sailing out to Father's house.

> The anchor I have lifted now;
>   My sails are floating free,

Amid the breeze that wafts my soul
  Beyond life's troubled sea.
I'm going where my Lord has gone,
  A mansion to prepare,
Where I through all eternity,
  May dwell in glory there.

A little child, between four and five years of age, on retiring knelt down to say her evening prayer and was heard to say,

"Dear Jesus, I thank you for being punished instead of me." She had heard her mother talking of Jesus taking our place. This incident inspired the hymn, "Instead of Me."

Good news from the gospel is sounding today;
I haste to receive it, how can I delay?
It tells me from bondage my soul may be free,
Through Jesus who suffered instead of me.

When informed of the death of a dear friend of Mrs. Currier's and mine we sat down and wept together, and these words flowed from my heart,

Only a little while pilgrims below,
Then to our fatherland home we shall go.

When I repeated the hymn to Mrs. Currier, she

immediately sang it to the music coming from her heart as the words did from mine. Both words and melody were written in less than half an hour.

After Mrs. Currier's consecration she was engaged to sing for six months in religious meetings in New York City; and in making the engagement had told them that she only sang gospel songs. They said that was enough, but on one occasion they asked her to sing at a certain large meeting something on the secular order, and when she reminded them of the agreement they asked her to stretch her conscience a little and think of it over night. She prayed for guidance and in the morning on taking out some music that had been packed away the first piece that struck her eye was "I Cannot Sing the Old Songs." She told me of the circumstance, and asked me to write a hymn telling why she could not sing the old songs. The result was "A New Song":

> I cannot sing the old songs,
>   For me their charm is o'er,
> My earthly harp is laid aside,
>   I wake its chords no more.
> The precious blood of Christ my Lord,
>   Has cleansed and made me free;
> And taught my heart a new song,
>   Of his great love to me.

During a series of meetings in Baltimore one evening Dr. Gilman of Johns Hopkins University called to ask Mrs. Currier to sing at a service where

workers of many denominations and creeds were
assembled. There were Jews, Romanists, and different Protestant churches represented. She was asked
for a hymn that would bring all closer together in
brotherly love, and spur them on to greater work.
No hymn could be found that fitted the case exactly, at least none in which so many creeds could
join; and so at her request was written "Let Him be
All in All."

From North to South, from East to West,
   Before our God above,
We meet to join our hearts and hands
   In one great work of love.

Then let us in our father's name,
   With holy reverence call,
Forgetting creed, forgetting self,
   Let him be "all in all."

A very dear friend, having passed through many
severe trials, persecutions and sorrows, came to me
and telling me of them said,

"God has led me all the way and has given me
'songs in the night.'" With the incident still fresh
in my mind I wrote the hymn entitled, "God
Leadeth:"

In paths that His wisdom and goodness prepare,
God leadeth his children along;
For he is our keeper and safe in His care,

God leadeth His children along;
Some through the water, some through the
flame,
Some through deep sorrow, but praised be His
name,
Where'er he leadeth, he giveth a song,
In the night season, and all the day long.

"I See the Light" has a beautiful history. A Boston
harbor pilot, as he lay dying, looked up and said to
those who watched by his bedside,

"I see the light." Supposing that he was dreaming
of familiar lights in the harbor, they asked,

"What light? Boston Light?"

"No," he replied.

"Highland Light?"

"No."

"Minot Light?"

The old pilot answered, "I see the Light of Glory,
now let the anchor go." With these words his spirit
passed over the bar, as his vessel had passed across
the harbor bar so many times, and there was no
moaning for him since his spirit was at rest.

I see the Light, 'tis coming,
    It breaks upon my soul;
It streams above the tempest,
    And ocean waves that roll.

From skies with clouds o'er shadowed,
    The mist dissolves away;
I see the Light that leadeth,
    To everlasting day.

With joy no words can utter,
   My heart is all aglow,
I see the Light of Glory,
   Now let the anchor go.

Among the many interesting letters, received of late, I select two or three that bear more directly upon the story of my life. From England during an evangelistic tour in the summer of 1900, Mr. Sankey wrote:

Dear Fanny:
   You are not forgotten and your name is often mentioned in connection with "Saved by Grace" in my services. We are keeping well and are just starting for Leeds, York, Sunderland, Berwick, Newcastle and Edinburgh, where large halls have been taken for our meetings. I quoted your beautiful lines of poetry recently in Birmingham:

      Oh, for an angel's harp to tell
      How much I love thee and how well!

They are fine and some of our mutual friends have written them down in their Bibles. I hope you are still as bright as a dollar, as you say.
                  Sincerely yours.
                        Ira D. Sankey.

I have spoken already of Imogene Hart, one of my

pupils in the Institution and a life-long friend. For a recent birthday she sent me the following greetings:

Dear Fanny:

I am the Imogene Hart who was one of your schoolmates at the Institution for the Blind in 1839. You were appointed to prepare me to join several classes that were well advanced in their studies. You taught me grammar, geography, and knitting. You also labored very hard to teach me to sing "second" in the hymn "Come Ye Disconsolate." I think you must have been greatly discouraged to hear my voice join the first sopranos after all your work to make me learn to sing alto.

I see by the "Tribune" that you are now eighty-five years old; and I congratulate you most heartily for the great good which you have all your life been able to accomplish through your beautiful hymns and carols—even writing up to this present day; and it makes me happy to know that you have always enjoyed good health and that you are still in the full enjoyment of life.

I was with you at the Institution less than three years, after which I developed a good voice and some musical ability. I am still able to sing a little although I shall be eighty years of age the first of next June. Sometimes I try my powers at composition; and I am going to send you some specimens of it. The "Polka Song" you must get some of your young lady friends to sing for you, so that you may judge that I keep up my good spirits.

Yours affectionately,
Imogene Hart

Mt. Vernon, N. Y.,
Jan. 14, 1901

Dear Friend of the Olden Time:

Most of our colleagues and associates of the forties and fifties have crossed the river; but, for some
reason, the ferryman has left you and me on this
side. We can count on our fingers nearly all of our
friends now living, who were with us at the Institution for the Blind from 1849 to 1854. With the
exception of the years just named I was a school-
master from the second Monday in November, 1835,
to the 10th of September last; and as I was teaching
more or less while in the Institution, I claim to
have been a teacher for sixty-four years and ten
months.

Since I retired last September, to occupy my time,
which for a while, "hung heavy on my hands," I
began to look over my old manuscripts and I will
copy a few lines from my diary, which was kept
during those years.

Nov. 21, 1850: Last evening one of our number
was converted at the 18th Street Church; and another (Fanny Crosby) at the 30th Street. I wish all of
our family were Christians; and then we would be a
happy family.

Do you remember that in 1851 a man came to
the Institution to get you to write for a new weekly
paper, to be called "The Saturday Emporium?" You
promised to write for him on the condition that I
should reply to you in the next number. You wrote
several poems, addressing me as Bertram, and signing
yourself 'Eurrilla.' I have in manuscript now my

answer to two of your poetic questions; one was

"Where shall the wounded spirit rest?"

But I can only remember the last two lines of
another question, and none of the one to which
these were part of the answer. To this second question, "What is earth's purest gem?" I wrote sixteen
four-line stanzas; and after sending you on a number of useless journeys, I concluded thus:

> Forgiveness is the brightest pearl,
> In all earth's diadem.

Wishing you long years more, health and happiness, I am,

Your lifelong friend,

T. D. Camp.

I am glad to be able to include a letter from Mr.
Faddoul Moghabghab, the real "Syrian Guest," whose
beautiful story has been written.

Miss Fanny Crosby,
Most beloved sister in Christ:

I am writing this letter with my Syrian pen, and
must therefore put the Syrian custom into practice
on such an occasion like this—Easter Week, "Jesus
Christ is risen"; "Is risen indeed." We use these
terms in Syria in place of your "Good morning," or
"Good evening," etc., especially on Sunday, Easter
day; and wheresoever we go or with whomever we

speak the first salutation is "Jesus Christ is risen today," and the reply "Is risen indeed."

Sister, though you are still in the body on this earth, you are always quoting the language of heaven above; and your thoughts are continually discovering new regions beyond the river. Oh, I imagine how happy you always feel; and I hope to have another chance of meeting you again upon this earth, because I always gain new inspiration from those whose mansions are already prepared by the "Shepherd of the Sheep"; but I am sure, if we cannot meet each other in this world, we shall meet in heaven.

I remain, yours in Christ,
Faddoul Moghabghab.

21

A Few Tributes

At the suggestion of several friends, I have finally concluded to add here a few of the tributes in song that kindred spirits have sent to me on various occasions. Between them and myself there has been a firm bond of sympathy and a keen appreciation of the kind words exchanged on birthdays and at Christmas time. I do not vouch for all of the things that these admiring and indulgent friends have said about me; I can only wish that all their words of praise were indeed well founded.

The first of these tributes was sent to me by a dear lady over the sea, whose name and sweet hymns have long been well known to our American people, Miss Frances Ridley Havergal. She and William F. Sherwin corresponded regularly for several years; and in one of her letters to my friend she inquired after "Fanny Crosby." Mr. Sherwin, in deference to my aversion to being called "the blind hymn writer," replied, "She is a blind lady, whose heart can see splendidly in the sunshine of God's love." Miss Havergal was deeply touched by this reply, and immediately wrote me a poem, which for thirty years has been a precious benediction to me. It is in grateful remembrance of the dear singer, who took a portion of her busy hours to write me from the depths of her heart that I quote a part of her poem here:

> Sweet blind singer over the sea,
> Tuneful and jubilant, how can it be,
> That the songs of gladness, which float so far,
> As if they fell from an evening star,
> Are the notes of one who may never see
> "Visible music" of flower and tree.
>
> How can she sing in the dark like this?
> What is her fountain of light and bliss?
>
> Her heart can see, her heart can see!
> Well may she sing so joyously!
> For the King himself, in his tender grace,
> Hath shown her the brightness of his face;
>
> Dear blind sister over the sea!
> An English heart goes forth to thee.
> We are linked by a cable of faith and song,
> Flashing bright sympathy swift along;
> One in the East and one in the West,
> Singing for him whom our souls love best,
>
> Sister! what will our meeting be,
> When our hearts shall sing and our eyes shall see?

From the time that I received the poem, from

which I have just quoted, until the death of the gifted English singer, seven years afterward, we frequently exchanged letters; and when "Bells at Evening" was published in 1897 I asked that her poem entire be included among my own works as a token of my appreciation of Miss Havergal's kindness.

On my birthday, March 24, 1893, Ira D. Sankey sent me the following beautiful poem:

> O friend beloved, with joy again
>   We hail thy natal day,
> Which brings you one year nearer home,
>   Rejoicing on the way.
>
> How fast the years are rolling on—
>   We cannot stay their flight;
> The summer sun is going down,
>   And soon will come the night.
>
> But you, dear friend, need fear no ill;
>   Your path shines bright and clear;
> You know the way, the truth, the life,
>   To you he's ever near.
>
> And when you pass from time away
>   To meet your Lord and King,
> In heaven you'll meet ten thousand souls,
>   That you have taught to sing.
>
> A few more years to sing the song
>   Of our Redeemer's love;
> Then by his grace both you and I
>   Shall sing his praise above.

To Fanny

The sun of life will darken,
  The voice of song will cease,
The ear to silence harken,
  The soul lie down in peace—
But with the trumpet's sounding,
  Ten thousand suns will glow,
And endless hymns abounding
  Like streams of love will flow.

Robert Lowry

March 24, 1897

For the last twenty years, or more, Mr. Hubert P. Main has sent me annually a poem for my birthday. Many of them were written in a humorous, or cheerful vein, like the following:

O Fanny, you're the worstest one,
  As ever yet I've knew,
You ask for things inopportune
  You du, you know you du!

It's every year along in March,
  When treetoads 'gin to roam,
You set me wilder than a hawk
  A howlin' for a *pome.*

I'm pestered, bothered, sick to death,
  I have so much tu du
On books, and services, and sich—
  I hev no time for you.

Still March the twenty-four comes round,
  In spite of earth or heaven;
And you keep coming also, tew,
  For now you're seventy-seven.

> Lord bless you, Fanny, this I'll say
> Since while my mill is runnin',
> I'm in dead earnest, too, and pray
> You will not think me funnin'.

One of these annual poems was addressed in the following unique lines:

> To Fanny Crosby, with a J,
> A poem for her natal day;
> Be gentle with it, postman, dear,
> You only cart it once a year;
> But hurry, hurry, please "cut sticks,"
> And leave at Ninth Street, Seventy-six.

On March 24, 1887, William J. Kirkpatrick wrote:

> Dear Fanny, I would send a line
> Of warm congratulation;
> And join the many friends that hail
> Your birthday celebration.
>
> To bless and cheer our rising race
> With songs of exultation,
> O, may your useful life be spared
> Another generation.

On my eighty-third birthday, in March, 1903, Dr.

John Gaylord Davenport of Waterbury sent me the following beautiful sonnet:

> Dear saint of God, another year has thrown
> Its light and shade along thine earthly way,
> And thou art lifting still thy tuneful lay
> And waking echoes still in souls unknown!
> How wondrously that melody has grown,
> Recalling those whose feet have gone astray
> And guiding toward the realms of perfect day
> Those whom the gracious Lord has made his own.
> Sing on, dear friend! Long teach us how to raise
> The note of aspiration and of love;
> Chanting the honors of our glorious King,
> Till all the world be jubilant with praise,
> And thine own music, keyed to bliss above,
> In every tongue of earth shall grandly ring.

During my summer visits at Assembly Park, New York, I have had the good fortune to meet a number of kindered spirits of note, among them Edmund Vance Cook, Miss Eliza E. Hewitt, and the late Alton Lindsay. The latter was a young man of abundant promise, but was taken from his host of friends by an early death. Mr. Cook is still young and composing those poetic strains that have cheered the hearts of so many. Miss Hewitt and I began to correspond as early as 1891, and at several birthdays she has written sweet poems for the informal receptions that are annually held at the office of Biglow

and Main in New York. In March, 1905, she sent
the following:

> The friends are forming a garland,
>   Fragrant and lovely and sweet,
> The roses and lilacs of friendship,
>   To lay at our loved one's feet;
>
> And while the fair chaplet they're twining,
>   May I bring a little flower,
> A forget-me-not, meek and lowly,
>   To add to the joys of the hour?
>
> This love-wreath is for our dear "Fanny,"
>   Whose heart is so young and so true,
> No wonder her songs, freely gushing,
>   Are as fresh as the morning dew!
>
> They sparkle with spring's happy sunshine,
>   They ripple like streams of delight,
> They flow from the rocks of the mountain,
>   They touch us with love's tender might.
>
> Because she sings of her Savior,
>   And his spirit tunes her lyre,
> Her work shall go on forever,
>   After she has been called up higher.
>
> So we'll gather round our "Fanny,"
>   With smiles and greetings sincere;
> May she have just the sweetest birthday
>   She has had for many a year.
>
> Then we'll all be happy with her,
>   And thank the dear Lord above,
> For sending us one of his angels
> To sing to us of his love.

Mr. Cook wrote in 1899:

Your brow is faded, poet, but we do not quarrel
With Time, since Time himself has brought
His recompense to you—the fadeless laurel
To crown your fadeless thought.

Your eyes are dark, O sister, but your inner vision
Is keener than a merely mortal sight;
Your poem of life has suffered no elision,
For all your life is light.

Your days are many, singer, but their goodly number
Has made you ever young,
Years are not years to you, nor can they cumber
The song your soul has sung.

Mr. John R. Clements, who has written many
sweet hymns, after the publication of my volume,
"Bells at Evening," in 1897, sent me the following
delightful lines:

Let chime again those "Bells at Evening,"
    Sounding rich and clear;
The music soothes and sweetly thrills,
    In harmonies so dear.

We fondly think of her who plays
    Deftly these even chimes,
And breathe a wish for length of days,
Good health and many rhymes.

At one of the Round Table mornings during my
stay at Assembly Park in 1899 Alton Lindsay recited the poem that is printed here in grateful remembrance of him:

O sweet-voiced singer of immortal songs,
Whose harmonies divine inspire the world
To nobler living and a loftier faith,
Arousing men to seek God's highest truth,
To praise his name and trust his promises;
And feel the Christ-love glow within the heart—
O, gentle singer, lean thy gracious head
And let me whisper low, as friend to friend,
A loving secret that I cannot keep.
Thy face, which mirror never shows to thee,
Itself is mirror of thy holy life,
Reflecting all the wealth of noble thought,
And all the beauty of thy purity.
The same glad joy which fills thy rapturous verse
Is like a flood of sunlight on thy brow,
Each hymn's calm message of perpetual trust
Is shining on thy placid countenance,
And all the hope of thy great mother-heart
Throbs ever in thy sweet and tender voice.
We thank our Heavenly Father for the boon
He gave to us in giving thee thy gift—
Thy gift of song which hath enriched the world.
Nor for the boon alone our praise we give,
For, like the magi, we behold a star,
Which guides us nearer to the Savior's side,
A radiant star—thy pure, unselfish life.

A Tribute

This year of nineteen hundred three
My muse comes nestling close to me,
And breathes these words quite tenderly:
'Our Fanny dear is eighty-three.'
So many years of usefulness!
So many years the world to bless!
So many years with pen and voice,
To make earth's weary ones rejoice!

Oh, what a blessed life is here—
The thought with love my bosom stirs;
Unselfish, patient, loving, kind,
And beautiful in heart and mind;
We read within the sacred Word:
'Blessed are those who fear the Lord,'
They strength shall gain; from day to day
On eagle's wings shall soar away.

Sweet blessings on our Fanny's head,
May paths be smooth where she shall tread;
Of life's best joys may she have plenty,
Who came to us in eighteen-twenty!
And may we meet at last in glory,
Together sing the dear old story,
That here we spread with best endeavor,
Hoping some precious sheaves to gather.

Harriet E. Jones

To Miss Fanny J. Crosby

(On her eighty-fifth birthday)

Unselfish singer of our heart's dear songs,
We pay to thee our tribute and our love.

Where man has wandered into grievous wrongs
Thy heart has gone, so like the Heart above!

O gracious singer, with the youthful years,
Thy lays have cheered in palace and in cot,
And now in memory's garden-plot appears
The fair and verdant flower forget-me-not!

Thy songs are planted in the Church's heart
To grow and bring forth fruit an hundred fold:
So may we also do our humble part
To honor thee, thou rarest heart of gold!

                              H. Adelbert White

22

Autobiographical Poems

During the last fifty years I have written a great many poems that might be called autobiographical. In the truest sense they record my own life history, because the most of them express some deep emotion; or recall some event in the life of my dearest friends; or revive some tender thought that I have not wished to pass unnoticed by those who do not know me so well. A number of them have been chosen for this book, not so much because of their literary merit, as because of the sentiments that they perpetuate. A few of them have been included in spite of the protests of modest souls whose worth happens therein to be duly recognized, but this is only one of the inadequate means that I have of expressing my gratitude and devotion to those who have paid me innumerable and tender attentions in times past and present.

Lines to My Mother

On My Birthday.

My birthday eve is gone, mother,
  And didst thou think of me?
Each moment while I counted o'er
  My thoughts wcre all on thee,

And oft I wished thee here, mother,
  Our social group to join;
For I long to clasp thine hand, mother,
  And in thy arms recline.

My birthday eve is gone, mother,
  The future who can know?
Oh, will my buoyant heart, as now,
  With gladness still o'erflow?

Or will its trembling strings, mother,
  Speak but a mournful tone?
And I, of all I love bereft,
  Weep wretched and alone?

My birthday eve is gone, mother,
  Friends gather round me now,
And they are sad, whene'er they mark
  A shadow on my brow.

They sing my favorite lays, mother,
  And many an hour beguile;
For they are dear as life to me—
  I live but in their smile.

To My Sister, Mrs. Julia Athington

(On the twentieth anniversary of her marriage)

Tell me, sister, does your memory
   Touch its lyre and murmur low
How your heart of joy was dreaming,
   Dreaming twenty years ago?
And the lovely wing of fancy,
   With your smile of beauty played,
While you stood before the altar
   In your bridal robe arrayed?

And to him who stood beside you,
   All your fondest hopes were given,
Vows were breathed and words were spoken,
   Read by seraph eyes in Heaven?
You have trod life's vale together,
   You have shared its good and ill,
Is your promise yet unbroken—
   Do you hold it sacred still?

Twenty years, and oh, how lightly,
   Time has touched you as he passed,
Hardly do you feel his autumn:
   It has brought no chilly blast.
Scarce a summer leaf has withered,
   Scarce a silver thread appears;
Few the traces age has left you,
   In the lapse of twenty years.

Sister, brother, I am with you,
   On your anniversary day,
With you in my thoughts and feelings,
   Wafted to your home away.
While the sunshine and the shadow
   Of the past you both review,

Pledge again your hearts' affection,
    And begin your lives anew.

Look to Him for strength and guidance,
    Who alone your souls can bless,
Ask His Spirit to be with you,
    Trust His love and faithfulness,
O, remember, life is fleeting,
    Let your future days be given
To an earnest, ardent seeking,
    For a home and rest in heaven!

1878

Reuben B. Currier and Mary E. Upham

(On their Wedding Day)

It is done, the words are spoken,
    Words that bind you heart to heart;
Whom the Lord hath joined together
    Neither life nor death can part.

Hope and friendship, joy and sunshine
    Hail you both on every side,
They are singing happy greeting
    To the bridegroom and the bride.

One in spirit, mind and purpose,
    You have loved each other long,
You have gathered souls for Jesus
    By your counsel and your song.

Unto Him we now commend you,
    Unto Him whose name is Love;
May the glory of His presence
    Rest upon you from above.

Father, Savior, Holy Spirit
  Bless these wedded souls we pray;
Make their future bright and cloudless
  As a rosy, summer day.

And when evening shadows gather,
  When their harvest work is done,
May they both go home rejoicing
  At the setting of the sun.

Sept. 7, 1904

Dedication of the Institution Chapel

Oh, thou omniscient, omnipresent Lord!
  Invisible, eternal God of all!
The vast creation trembles at thy word,
  And at thy footstool nations prostrate fall.

Thy throne is fixed above the starry frame;
  Yet thou in earthly temples lov'st to dwell;
The humble spirit thou wilt not disdain,
  The wounded heart thy balm divine dost heal.

Father, we humbly supplicate thy grace,
  May thy benignant smile on us be given,
Thy blessing rest upon this sacred place,
  Thine earthly house, we trust, the gate of heaven.

Here will we listen to thy holy word;
  Light on our path, thus, may its precepts be;
Here shall the voice of praise and prayer be heard—
  Ourselves, our all, we dedicate to thee.

1841

On a Child Kneeling

His little hands were meekly clasped,
  And to that cheek so fair,

A ringlet carelessly had strayed,
And lightly lingered there,

Beneath those silken lids that dropped,
Were eyes serenely bright;
An infant kneels, and angels gaze
With rapture at the sight.

Well may they strike their golden harps,
And swell their songs of praise;
An infant kneels in artless strains
Its feeble voice to raise.

Oh, what a lesson! if a child
So innocent must kneel,
Should not our sinful time-seared hearts
A deep contrition feel?

How often from a little child
May we a lesson learn!
Remind us of our wanderings,
And urged to quick return.

1842

The Wish

I ask—but not the glittering pomp—
Of wealth and pageantry;
Nor splendid dome: a rural cot
My domicile shall be.

'Tis not to mingle with the gay,
The opulent, and proud;
'Tis not to court the flattering smile
Of an admiring crowd.

I ask a heart—a faithful heart—
Congenial with mine own,

Whose deep, unchanging love shall burn
   For me, and me alone:

A heart in sorrow's cheerless hour
   To soften every care;
To taste with me the sweets of life,
   And all its ills to share.

Thus linked by friendship's golden chain,
   Ah, who more blessed than we;
Unruffled as the pearly stream
   Our halcyon days would be.

1842

I'll Think of Thee

(Words and Music)

I'll think of thee at that soft hour,
   When fade the parting hues of day;
And on each grove and woodland bower
   The balmy gales of summer play.

When night around her mantle throws,
   And stars illume the deep blue sea,
When wearied nature seeks repose,
   Oh, then, I'll dream, I'll dream of thee.

When from the East the morning breaks;
   And night's dark shadows glide away;
When nature from her slumber wakes
   To hail with joy the opening day.

When sweetly bursting on the ear,
   The tuneful warbler's note of glee,
I'll fondly fancy thou art near
   To touch the light guitar for me.

1842

An Address
(Recited while on the tour through New York, 1843)

The deep blue sky, serenely light,
    On which your eyes with rapture gaze;
Where stars unveil their mellow bright,
    And God his wondrous power displays;

The gushing fount, whose glassy breast,
    Reflects the parting hues of day,
Nature in robes of verdure drest,
    The opening buds, the flowerets gay;

The lofty hills, the greenwood bowers—
    Though fair these rural scenes appear,
On them to gaze must ne'er be ours:
    These orbs, alas! they cannot cheer.

But, yet, instruction's nobler light,
    Sheds on our mental eye its ray;
We hail its beams with new delight,
    And bid each gloomy thought away.

To us the Lord kind friends has given,
    Whose names we ever shall revere,
Recorded in the book of heaven,
    Shall their munificence appear.

But, while our sunny moments fly,
    Unsullied by a shade of care,
For those, like us bereft, we sigh,
    And wish they, too, our joys might share.
1843

Song of the Greek Exile

Farewell, guitar! this faltering hand
    Will touch thy trembling chords no more.

Far from my lovely, native land,
  I languish on a distant shore;
From Grecia's isle forever torn,
  A captive exile, now I mourn.

Farewell, guitar! another hand
  Will wake thy trembling chords for me,
And in my own dear native land
  Recall my favorite melody:
The land where minstrels poured their lays,
  Where dwelt the bard of bygone days.

Oh, might I find at last a grave
  In thee, my happy, happy isle!
The mournful cypress o'er me wave,
  And wild flowers sadly on me smile;
There, bosom friends, and kindred dear
  Would to my memory drop a tear.

1843

Reflections on the Closing Year

'Twill soon be gone—the wailing night wind drear
Chants her sad requiem to the closing year:
'Twill soon be gone—the brilliant starry night
In silent eloquence repeats the strain.

'Twill soon be gone—the placid queen of night
O'er its departure sheds her mellow light.
Oh, time, what art thou? who thy course may stay?
Not ours the past nor future, but today.

Hark! hark! the distant peal of yonder bell,
In measured tones the midnight hour doth tell.
Old year, thy reign is past; we bid adieu
To thee, and usher in the new.

I'll to my couch, and dream the hours away,
'Till fair Aurora opes the gates of day:
But ere I go, dear friends, on you I call:
"A happy new year" is my wish to all.
1843

To Rusticus

(In answer to the lines "My Heart Is Weary")

Oh, why forgotten wouldst thou sleep
    Beneath some lonely tree?
Has this bright world, so beautiful,
    No sunny spots for thee?
Thou sayest thy heart is weary—
    Hath sorrow swept its strings?
Its every tone of buried hopes
    Some sad remembrance brings?

Go where the gushing fountain
    Leaps from the rock-bound hill;
And let its quiet murmurs
    Thy heart's wild throbbing still;
Scorn not the humble daisy,
    Nor lily's drooping form;
For, trust me, thou wilt never find
    A rose without a thorn!
August, 1847

Time Chronicled in a Skull

A skull was once placed in my hand and I placed a
watch inside it. The thoughts that came to me then were
afterwards written out in a poem.

Why should I fear it? Once the pulse of life
Throbbed in these temples, pale and bloodless now.
Here reason sat enthroned, its empire held

O'er infant thought and thought to action grown:
A flashing eye in varying glances told
The secret workings of immortal mind.
The vital spark hath fled, and hope, and love,
And hatred—all are buried in the dust,
Forgotten, like the cold and senseless clay
That lies before me: such is human life.
Mortals, behold and read your destiny!
Faithful chronometer, which now I place
Within this cavity with faltering hand,
Tell me how swift the passing moments fly!
I hear thy voice and tremble as I hear,
For time and death are blended—awful thought.
Death claims its victim. Time, that once was his,
Bearing him onward with resistless power,
Must in the vast eternity be lost.
Eternity, duration infinite!
Ages on ages roll unnumbered there;
From star to star the soul enraptured flies,
Drinking new beauties, transports ever new,
Casting its crown of glory at his feet,
Whose word from chaos to existence called
A universe; whose hand omnipotent
Controls the storms that wake the boundless deep,
"And guides the planet in its wild career."
1848

He Goes Before You

(Matthew xxvii: 7; Middle Clause)

O troubled ones, why thus repine,
And yield to care and sorrow?
Though clouds may veil your sky today,
The sun will shine tomorrow.

Chorus:
>   He lives again, your Savior lives;
>   His banner still is o'er you,
>   Then trust the words the angel said:
>   Behold he goes before you!

>   He goes before to cheer the path
>   Your weary feet are treading;
>   And all along, his gentle hand
>   A feast of love is spreading.

>   O troubled ones, be not afraid;
>   Press on with firm endeavor
>   To meet with joy your risen Lord,
>   And dwell with him forever.

An Address to Henry Clay

On the occasion of his visit to the New York Institution
for the Blind.

It comes, it swells, it breaks upon the ear;
Millions have caught the spirit stirring sound.
And we with joy, with transport uncontrolled,
Would in the chorus of our city join:
Thou noblest of the noble, welcome here!
Noble in high born deeds of spotless fame—
Yes, in behalf of those who o'er us watch,
We bid thee welcome to this lovely spot,
Our peaceful home, where kindred souls are knit
In one sweet bond of friendship unalloyed.
It is not ours thy lineaments to trace,
The intellectual brow, the flashing eye.
Those glance the language of the soul portrays.
But fancy's busy hand the picture draws,
And with a smile, the glowing sketch presents

To hearts that with anticipation throb.
How have we longed to meet thee, thou whose
    voice,
In eloquence resistless, like a spell,
Holds e'en a nation captive to its powers!
Well may Columbia of her son be proud.
Firm as a rock, amid conflicting storms,
Thou by her side hast ever fearless stood,
With truth thy motto, principle thy guide.
And thou canst feel as rich a gem is thine,
As ever graced the loftiest monarch's brow:
A nation's honor and a nation's love.
O'er Ashland veiled in winter's cheerless night,
Ere long will steal the gentle breath of spring;
And thou wilt sit among the shades embowered
Of ancient trees, whose giant branches wave
Around the quiet home thou lovest so dear.
The winding streamlet on whose pearly breast
The crescent moon reflects her silver light,
Will murmur on; and when the blushing morn
Calls nature from a soft and dewy sleep
The birds will glad thee with their gushing songs,
So sweetly caroled to the newborn day.
Once more, illustrious statesman, welcome here!
Language can do no more, these trembling lips
To our emotions utterance cannot give.
Yet we would ask, ere thou from us depart,
Oh, let thine accents greet each anxious ear.
Speak, we entreat thee, but one parting word,
That in the secret chambers of the heart
May live the memory of its thrilling tones,
When he who uttered them is far away.
1848

Influenza

(A play on the names of the Managers)

Now list ye, dear friends, I've a story to tell,
If I mistake not, 'twill please you right well.
You all recollect what a scene of confusion
Once reigned for a week in our good Institution,
For a being with manners exceedingly rude
On our sanctum sanctorum had dared to intrude;
His horrible grip threw us all in a frenzy—
He'd a singular name, he was called Influenzy.
Though treated with Clements, yet all would not
    do,
He fearlessly seized on a Chamberlain, too,
Who struggled in vain, for the wretch held him fast,
And catching his voice cried, "I have you at last."
Our Board of Directors thought best to convene:
    The result of their counsel will shortly be seen;
Our president, Phelps, Mr. Allen, and Moore
Declared such a thing ne'er happened before;
And the best they could do was at once to expel
    him,
And appoint in due form a committee to tell him;
And as for his principles all must agree
He ought to be ruled by a K-i-n-g—
But said Mr. Shelden: "My friend, Mr. Jones,
I move that the creature be pelted with stones."
"No, no," said the other, who thoughtfully stood,
"For then he might easily fly to a Wood,
Besides, I consider such treatment too harsh,
But, Cased in a Schell, let him sink in a Marsh,
With a Cross-bee around him to torture and try
    him,
And remember that Beers of all kinds we deny
    him,
We let him Thurst, on, am I right, Mr. Murray?

Whatever we do, must be done in a hurry:
At times he is in a Brown study, they say;
Now, I would suggest that we take him, to-Day.'
"To-Day, by all means," Mr. Murray replied.
With that Influenzy stood close by his side,
But just as an arm o'er his shoulder he put,
By Robertson Welch he was bound hand and foot;
Unlike to most captives his dungeon was spacy,
His judge, I am told, was remarkable Gracie,
His fate, I am sure, I have no wish to deplore it,
And I've heard since like a martyr he bore it.
1850

The Rover

I am free as the mountain breezes wild,
   My sable plumes that wave;
And my heart is as gay as the heart of the bird,
   And my spirit is bold and brave.

My trusty sword, like a faithful friend,
   Hangs glittering at my side;
And I steer my bark with a daring hand
   On the breast of the furious tide.

I love to look on the frowning sky,
   When the vivid lightnings flash;
And the tempest shrieks at the dead of night,
   And the rolling thunders crash.

I have stood on the deck of my noble craft,
   And watched its shattered sail;
I have seen its mast in pieces dashed,
   Hang quivering in the gale.

But think ye my cheeks were pale with dread,
   Or my blood grew cold and chill?
There was music for me in the mad winds' mirth,
   And my heart beats fearless still.

I have stood in the battle's foremost ranks,
　When the booming shots came fast;
And the light grew dim in the warrior's eye,
　And the valiant were breathing their last.

I never quailed 'neath a tyrant's glance,
　A slave I have scorned to be;
They have sought my life, they have sought in vain,
　I am free—I am free—I am free!
1849

The Captive

The deep-toned bell, from Linder's lofty tower,
With awful peal proclaims the midnight hour;
And spectres grim, in robes of ghastly white,
Come forth to wander through the gloom of night.

They move with noiseless tread, that ghostly train,
Low, muttering sounds convulse the trembling frame,
The eye revolts in terror from the sight,
The blood congeals, the cheek grows deathly white.

That ancient tower for centuries hath stood,
The scene of barbarous cruelty and blood:
The hapless victim, doomed to torturing pain,
Though innocent, for mercy pleads in vain,
Within those hated walls her accents never came.

Blind superstition wields its scepter there,
And fiends in human form its tenants are;
The mangled wretch with frantic joy they see,
And laugh exulting at his agony.

Within a deep and loathsome vault, confined
For years, a captive, hath Alvero pined;

A youth of noble origin is he
In this abode of guilt and misery.

Why is he doomed a wretched life to spend?
Oh, death to him would be a welcome friend;
Pale and distorted are his features now,
And grief sits silent on his lofty brow.

Say what his crime? ask of that tyrant band
That with malignant looks around him stand;
Fell murderers, hold! ye stern, accursed throng,
Hold, or high heaven will yet avenge his wrong.

'Tis done, 'tis done! I see the quivering dart:
The life blood gushes from Alvero's heart,
A deep convulsive sigh his bosom yields—
Hark! hark! methinks a kindred name he breathes.

Oh, Evaline, far, far from thee I die,
Would thou coulds't hear my last expiring sigh;
Would that my head were pillowed on thy breast,
How calm, how peaceful, could I sink to rest.

If those who dwell in yon celestial sphere
Forget not those they loved on earth so dear;
If mortal's sorrows they, perchance, may see,
My faithful spirit shall thy guardian be.

A groan—another—he has passed away
To the bright regions of eternal day,
The affrighted raven screams and flaps her wings,
Night's mournful wind the captive's requiem sings.

The Presumptuous Mouse

(Written from an actual incident)

Dear friends, recieve attentively
A strange account of Mr. C.

With your permission I'll relate—
Though you may smile at his sad fate—
How while reposing on his bed,
And airy thoughts flit through his head,
A weary mouse house hunting crept,
Close to the pillow where he slept;
But there not feeling quite at ease,
And wishing much himself to please,
He looked with grave and thoughtful air
On Mr. C's dishevelled hair.
"Ah, here's the station I like best,"
Said he, "and here I'll build my nest.
This scalp conceals a poet's brain,
So here till morning I'll remain,
Perhaps the muse will me inspire,
And if she tune her magic lyre,
I'll to the world proclaim that we,
That mice, like men, may poets be."
Our hero thus descanted long
On love, and poesy and song;
While now and then a gentle squeal
His vocal powers would reveal.
His train of eloquence it broke,
For Mr. C, perplexed awoke,
And starting up—"I do declare
There's something scraping in my hair;
A light; a light; what shall I do?"
At this the mouse, alarmed, withdrew;
And had he not, I'm certain, death
Had stopped, ere long, his little breath.
1850

To a Friend
(Cynthia Bullock)

When wilt thou think of me?
When the vesper bell is pealing,
And its distant sounds are stealing
Softly on the listening ear,
Breathing music sweet and clear;
When in prayer on bended knee,
Wilt thou then remember me?

When wilt thou think of me?
When the twilight fades away,
And the bird hath ceased its lay,
And the quiet evening shade
Lingers in the silent glade;
When thy thoughts are wandering free,
Wilt thou then remember me?

When wilt thou think of me?
When thy gentle heart is crushed,
And its sweetest tones are hushed;
When upon some faithful breast,
Thou wouldst lull thy grief to rest,
Then in whispers soft to thee
I would say, remember me.
1850

"Hope On, Hope Ever"

"Hope on, hope ever"—earth is not so drear,
Nor life a comfortless and empty dream;
The darkest clouds that gather o'er us here,
Are not the harbingers we sometimes deem;
For lo, how brilliant the returning ray,
As one by one their shadows pass away!

"Hope on, hope ever"—Is thy heart bereft
Of all that rendered life once dear to thee?
Amid the wreck the quenchless spark is left,
Whose light, though feeble, shall thy beacon be.
Though death's cold hand some kindred tie may
    sever,
Still let thy motto be, "Hope on, hope ever."

"Hope on, hope ever"—weary and oppressed,
Care's pallid seal stamped on thy sunken cheek;
There is a haven of eternal rest
Whose sacred joy no mortal tongue can speak;
Look upward in thine hour of dark despair:
Hope points to heaven, and drops her anchor there.

A Reverie

Under the boughs of the waving trees,
Wooing the breath from a passing breeze,
Gathering daisies pure and sweet,
Far from the noisy crowded street,
There would I sit through the long, long day,
Dreaming the golden hours away;
Dreaming of pleasures that fancy brings
'Neath the silken folds of her airy wings,
Till my heart beats quick and I feel the glow
Of friendship's smile in the long ago.

Down where the ocean billows swell,
And over and over their story tell,
Down where the distant breakers roar,
And I hear their voice on the sandy shore,
There would I be when the sunset hue
Fades in the depths of the waters blue;
There would I roam when the shadows creep

over the face of the mighty deep,
And the moon looks down from her saintly
  bower
With a hallowed light on that lone, lone hour.

Sabbath Evening

Lo, the setting sun is stealing
  Softly through the clustering vines;
On the spirit sweet peace sealing,
  As this Sabbath day declines.

Lovely spot, oh, sacred hour,
  Day of all our days the best,
Weakening the tempter's power,
  Pointing to the promised rest.

While we watch thy fading splendor,
  Thou adorner of the skies,
May we all our hearts surrender
  To the God who bade thee rise.

Our Country

Our country, unrivalled in beauty,
And splendor that cannot be told,
How lovely thy hills and thy woodlands,
Arrayed in the sunlight of gold.
The eagle, proud king of the mountain,
Is soaring majestic and free;
Thy rivers and lakes in their grandeur
Roll on to the arms of the sea.

Our country, the birthplace of freedom,
The land where our forefathers trod,
And sang in the aisles of the forest
Their hymns of thanksgiving to God.

Their bark they had moored in the harbor,
No more on the ocean to roam;
And there in the wilds of New England
They founded a country and home.

Our country, with ardent devotion,
In God may thy children abide;
In him be the strength of the nation,
His laws and His counsel to guide.
Our banner—that time honored banner—
That floats in the ocean's bright foam,
God keep it unsullied forever,
Our standard, our union, our home.

A Tribute

(To the memory of our dead heroes)

To arms! to arms! We remember well
   That wild, tumultuous cry,
When our country rang with clash and clang
   Of swords that were lifted high;
For the king of war, on his fiery steed,
   Shot flame from his flashing eye.

The eagle screamed as he flapped his wings,
   And soared to his rock-girt nest,
And the ocean moaned, as he heard the sound
   Far, far on his heaving breast.

To arms! to arms! and defend your cause!
   In the cannon's boom was heard;
And the clarion swelled its pealing note,
   Till every soul was stirred;
And our gallant brave from the homes they loved
   Went forth at their country's word.

Side by side on the battlefield,
  With loyal hearts and true,
Side by side they fought and died
  For the old red, white and blue.

And now we stand on the sacred spot,
  Where we laid them down to sleep;
And we touch the chords of memory's harp,
  And linger awhile to weep.
With grateful hearts and reverent lips,
  We tell of their deeds of fame;
And cover them over with fair young flowers
  That whisper their honored name.

Their work is done; and from year to year
  We hallow their graves anew;
Their work is done, and our banner bright
  Unfurled to the breeze we view;
And we look with pride on the Stars and Stripes,
  That were saved by the Boys in Blue.

What the Old Year Saw

The moon looked down from a cloudless sky,
On the white and crispy snow;
And one by one the hours went by,
While I heard the wild winds blow.
I thought of those who were toiling hard,
Their burden of life to bear;
I thought of the homes that were dark and cold,
And the little ones shivering there;

Then I looked again at the queenly moon,
As she walked in her path of light;
And I prayed from the depths of my inmost soul,
"Lord, pity the poor tonight."
While thus I mused by myself alone,

Watching the embers glow,
A form stole in; he was bent with age,
And his locks were white as snow.

"You wonder," he said, and his voice was weak;
"You wonder to find me here.
But much have I seen that I fain would tell,
And then I must bid you a long farewell
For I am the old, old year.
Yes, much have I seen of good and ill,
Of pleasure and sorrow, too.
Take heed to my counsel where'er you go.

"Be kind to the erring and soothe their woe,
As God has been kind to you.
I saw a youth in an evil hour
Beguiled by the tempting bowl;
And he deeply drank of its baneful dregs,
That burned to his very soul;
And I saw him won by a loving word:
Reclaimed from his reckless ways;

"And only this morning I heard him say
'To Jesus be all his praise':
I saw a wife by her husband's side,
And her hand he warmly pressed;
I heard her singing a cradle song,
And hushing her babe to rest.
But the demon entered their peaceful home,
And clouded her fair young brow,

"For he, who had promised her lot to bless,
Had made it a thorny wilderness,
Forgetting his marriage vow.
The demon entered that peaceful home,
And stalked with remorseless tread;
But she bore it all with woman's trust

Till her last, last hope had fled—
Till the child of her love, by an angel borne,

"Went home where no tears are shed.
The father gazed on the pale, sweet face
Of the babe, so still and fair;
In its little hand was an opening bud:
Dear mamma had placed it there.
He stood and gazed on its pale, sweet face,
And his noble nature stirred.
And the man of God from a mission came

"To read from the Holy Word.
He read of the tears the Savior shed
O'er the grave where Lazarus slept;
A chord was touched in the father's breast,
And he bowed his head and wept.
'Twas a touching scene, aye, a touching scene,
I remembered it many a day,
How he knelt him down by his stricken wife,

"And asked the goodly man to pray:
But still he knelt with a firm resolve
And promised then and there
By the grace of God and the pastor's prayer
He never would drink again.
I have seen the altars with mourners filled,
And they gave their hearts to God:
I have seen them look with a shudder, back

"To the path they once had trod.
And many a picture bright I've seen
At merry Christmas time;
When the bells rang out, 'Good will to men,'
With clear and silver chime.
Good will to men through the Savior's birth—
Oh, precious truth sublime.

And now I have come to my closing hour,

"My task is well nigh done;
And 1880 must soon give place to 1881.
Faster and faster the moments bring
The end of my brief career;
I shall soon be gone, and a happy song
Will welcome the newborn year.
'Do good, do good, for the Master's sake'
Is the message I leave to all;

"Be sure you are ready whene'er he comes,
To answer the Master's call."
And the old year passed from my wondering eyes
Through the veil of light serene;
And a record he bore to eternity's shore
Of all that he had heard and seen.

For the Dedication of a Church

Eternal God of ages,
And source of boundless love,
We praise thee for thy mercies,
That crown us from above.
Our pleasant task completed
With joyful eyes we see;
And now our earthly temple
We consecrate to thee.

Accept our cheerful offering,
And may this holy day,
Be one whose tender memory
will never fade away.
O, fill us with thy Spirit,
And may our faith behold
The glory cloud descending,
And resting, as of old.

Receive our cheerful offering
From loyal hearts and true,
Who labored, prayed and trusted,
Although in number few.
Thy promise gave us courage;
And now with joy we see
Our work begun, continued,
And ended, Lord, in thee.

To Our Mother on Her Eighty-ninth Birthday

Tender thoughts their spell are weaving,
  Hallowed memories round us twine,
'Tis the birthday of our mother,
  And her years are eighty-nine;
Years that fraught with many changes
  Came and went as flies a dream,
Came and went as speeds an arrow,
  Or a meteor's flashing beam.
But her eye retains a lustre,
  And her face a genial glow,
That illumines every feature,
  With the smile of long ago;
And we fancy that the autumn
  Of her life is waning now,
And forget the winter's snowflakes,
  Resting gently on her brow.
Mother's birthday, and her children
  Three in number, all are here,
From the sunny past recalling
  Words of love and still revere.
Four grandchildren grace our circle,
  Breathing wishes kind and true,
Mother's joy to make still brighter,
  See! her great-grandchildren, too.

But our hearts must pause a moment
  O'er the missing ones to mourn:
Where are William, Lee, and Byron,
  Will those dear ones ne'er return?
Will our mother's birthday never
  Bring them back to us again?
We shall listen for their footsteps,
  We shall watch for them in vain;
But the voice of him who suffered,
  And hath risen from the tomb,
Gives us comfort in our sorrow,
  Whispers hope beyond the gloom.
O, the bliss of sweet reunion,
  When the last wild storm is o'er,
When our souls have braved the tempest,
  And our bark has reached the shore.
Mother's birthday! God reward her
  For her gentle, patient care,
May he light the path before her
  Is the burden of our prayer;
And may all who now are gathered
  On this happy eve so bright,
Meet at last beyond the river,
  Where they never say, "Good night!"

1888

Our Beautiful Baby Clare

(Dedicated to the memory of my little niece,
Clare Hope, daughter of Mr. Albert E. and Mrs.
Clara O. Morris, who passed away July 1, 1891.)

Silently came the angel,
A white-robed angel fair,
And carried away our darling,

Our beautiful baby Clare,
Carried her home to the songland
To dwell in its blissful bowers,
And play with the infant cherubs,
Who gather its fadeless flowers.

Silently came the angel,
And whispered in accents clear,
"I bring you a balm of comfort
Your sorrowing hearts to cheer;
God spareth the wife and mother
In answer to earnest prayer,
But taketh where she may follow
Her beautiful baby Clare."

We know not the unseen future,
'Tis wisely from us concealed,
We know not the way before us,
But this hath our Lord revealed:
Through clouds that may seem the darkest
There shineth a radiance bright,
That maketh each tear a jewel
To sparkle in God's own light.

Oh, let not our hearts be troubled,
But trust our Redeemer's love,
Who kindly now is preparing
A mansion for us above;
Not here is our home, but yonder,
Not here is our rest, but there,
Where Jesus our Lord hath beckoned
Our beautiful baby Clare.

Though Papa will miss his darling,
   So gentle and pure and sweet,

And "Dan-ma" will hear no longer
 The tread of her tiny feet,
Oh, think of the blest reunion,
 No parting nor pain is there,
But safe in the arms of Jesus
 Is our beautiful baby Clare.

A Tribute

(To the Memory of Col. Samuel B. Sumner)

It cannot be, and yet the low sad moan
Of midnight winds with melancholy tone
A requiem chant, that from his tomb they bore;
Weep gentle muse for Sumner is no more.
Yet he doth live, no heart so kind as he,
So brave and noble can forgotten be.
Immortal genius and heroic fame,
With sparkling jewels, crown our poet's name:
True to the land of his ancestral birth,
He sang her praise in strains of peerless worth;
Held up her flag in battle's dread affray,
Through many a weary march and toil-worn
 day;
And on the field, as oft his comrades tell,
He did his duty, and he did it well.
His end was calm as evening's sunset glow,
How like to hers, who three short years ago
Looked in his face, then closed her tranquil eye,
And in that look bade those she loved "good-bye."
Perchance 'twas she who came on pinions bright
Or floating downward on a beam of light,
Drew him away to that sweet realm above,
Life's great beyond, its paradise of love.

O, hearts bereaved, there is a morn of peace,
When every wave and every storm shall cease;
A world of joy without one throb of pain,
A home of bliss where loved ones meet again,
O kindred spirit, rest; they work is o'er,
Thy lips are mute, thy harp resounds no more,
Yet will its echoes come at hush of night,
When silver stars unveil their pensive light,
And we shall hope in heaven with thee to dwell,
Where they who meet shall never say farewell.
1891

In Eden's Vale of Flowers

(Affectionately dedicated to my nephew and niece Mr. and Mrs. William Tait, on the death of their infant son, Morris William Tait, August 1893.)

I know you are sad and lonely,
    Through tears I hear you say:
From Papa, Mamma and Mary
    Our boy has gone away:
Our boy like the ivy clinging
    Around each breaking heart,
Our dear little baby, Morris,
    'Tis hard from him to part."

Oh, yes, but your precious darling
    In yonder home of rest,
Is "safe in the arms of Jesus,"
    "Safe on his gentle breast";
And, oh, could the veil be lifted,
    That hides your babe so fair,
How soon you would lose forever
    The cross that now you bear!

I know of a beautiful garden,
   Where he, our Lord and King,
Came down with the blush of the morning
   The dew of love to bring;
And, seeing a pure white lily,
   Too frail for earthly bowers,
He carried it in his bosom
   To Eden's vale of flowers.

Oh, think what a radiant picture
   What joy its light portrays,
Our Savior is tender hearted,
   And kind in all his ways;
Though sometimes the paths before us,
   With clouds are dark and dim,
'Tis only that he may draw us
   In closer bonds to him.

Not so far is the silent river,
   Not far is the golden shore,
Not long till we shall gather,
   Where parting comes no more;
There music from harps and voices,
   Rolls on in tuneful strain,
Where Papa, Mamma and Mary
   Will clasp their boy again.

A Birthday Tribute

Unselfish, noble, true and constant friend,
Take thou my greeting on thy birthday morn,
That breaks resplendent from the orient sky,
With hope and promise of a golden year,
Sweet as the echo of the crystal bells,
That sing responsive to the angels' song;

I hear the music of the sacred nine,
For they would usher in this welcome hour,
And waft this tribute on the vernal breeze.
One little sparkling gem today I bring,
A gem whose lustre will forever shine,
I found it in an urn by friendship sealed,
And closely guarded by her watchful eye;
Her gift and mine to crown thy natal morn;
Accept it then, and may it breathe for thee
In words I would not have the power to speak
What thou hast been and what thou art to me.

A Reverie

The winds a carol murmur, soft and low,
While silver stars, that gem the arch of night
In answering tones, repeat the choral strain:
Sleep on, O minstrel, calm be thy repose,
Pure as thy spirit, guileless as thy heart;
May golden dreams of past and future years,
Of deeds accomplished, laurels nobly won,
Beguile thy slumber with their magic power,
And bear thee onward to the classic vales,
Where thou in thought hast wandered o'er and o'er,
Hast laved thy brow in sweet Arcadian springs,
And caught the music of Apollo's lyre:
Sleep on, O minstrel, angels guard thy rest,
Till in her chariot drawn by flaming steeds,
Comes the fair goddess of the blushing morn,
And in her beauty smiling bids thee wake.
1903

Night and Morning

Lo, the vesper hour hath flown,
Voices of the dewy night

Hold me captive with delight
To their mystic tone.

Strangely wild, yet passing sweet,
   Falls their music on my ear,
   While a fountain soft and clear
Murmurs at my feet.

Ah, too soon the moments fly,
   Now the bird his nest forsakes
   And the rosy morning breaks
From the Orient sky.

1903

On the Dedication of a Church Organ

Thou in whose chords the soul of music dwells,
Tuned by a master hand, awake, awake,
And in these temple walls where thou dost stand,
Peal forth thy first glad song of joyful praise
To him the great Creator of us all,
The Mighty Lord, the Universal King.

Thou art our offering, unto him alone
We dedicate thee on this Sabbath day,
And while we listen to thy thrilling tones,
Now soft, now swelling with ecstatic bliss,
Oh, may our voices blend with one accord,
And faith directed may our spirits rise;
Beyond the clouds and look within the veil.

Accept, O gracious Lord, the gift we bring,
Receive the tribute of our grateful love,
And when, as now, we gather in thy name,
Beyond this organ for thy worship made;
Behold the singers, and their song inspire.
Here, may the smile of gentle peace abide,
And here the brightness of thy glory shine.

1905

A Pleasant Reminiscence

(School for the Blind, Wethersfield Ave.,
        Hartford, Conn.)

There's a day that comes from the sunny
    past,
Where it lives in friendship's bowers;
And it whispers soft of a hallowed scene
In the early spring when the hills were
    green
And we met for a few brief hours.

'Tis a day long past, but remembered yet
When I stood in your home so dear;
I can see you all as I saw you then,
I can feel the clasp of each hand again
And your welcome words I hear.

O friends beloved, 'tis a golden chain
That binds us heart to heart,
'Twas woven in light where angels sing
And the roses bloom in eternal spring,
And its links no power can part.

And oft as I muse and my brow is fanned
By a breath from the passing gales,
Though weary my spirit at times may be,
How restful the pleasure that flows to me.
While reading your "Talks and Tales."

To Brother and Sister Cobham

The noble deed you both have done,
　　O precious friends of mine,
A star has added to your crown,
　　That on your brow will shine.
You did it in the Master's name,
　　And yet you little knew
That angel eyes were looking down
　　From yonder arch of blue.

Three youthful workers for the Lord
　　Were brought at your behest,
And in your sunlit home they found
　　The bliss of tranquil rest.
You gave them kindly words of cheer,
　　And strewed their path with flowers;
They heard the carol of the birds
　　In nature's rural bowers.

They bounded o'er the rock girt hills
　　And paused awhile to see,
The Allegheny, flowing on,
　　Majestic, grand and free;
Then turning back they sought again,
　　Your dwelling in the grove,
And to the light guitar they sang
　　Glad songs of grateful love.

And when we gathered round your board,
　　With tempting viands blest,
You did not leave the driver out,
　　But called him with the rest;
He took his place, the moments passed
　　In social converse sweet;
We ate and drank, and praised the Lord
　　For such a dear retreat.

But then the evening time drew near,
   We saw the shades descend,
And with a sigh of fond regret,
   We parted, friend with friend;
The light guitar, the choral song.
   Will in our memory dwell,
Till we, in glory, clasp our hands,
   No more to say farewell.

O precious friends, your noble deeds
   Will never, never die,
Behold and read in gilded lines
   Their message in the sky.
The Lord is with you, fear ye not,
   Though pilgrims here ye roam,
He'll bring you safe where those you love
   Will sing your Welcome Home.

1905

Chautauquan Greeting

(Dedicated to the Round Table,
August 10, 1906)

In these classic wilds of beauty,
   In our summer land so dear,
Crowned with blessings rich and boundless
   We have gathered year by year.

From the village and the hamlet,
   From the city's crowded streets,
In our summer home so tranquil,
   We are spared again to meet.

Hail, Chautauquan sons and daughters,
   Swell the chorus; let it break
O'er the forest and the mountain,
   O'er the waves of Tully Lake.

Like Minerva, rich in wisdom,
  Dropping words like gentle dew,
Still our President is with us,
  And her magic wand we view.

While our noble, kind director,
  Warmly as in years before,
Gives to each a cordial welcome
  To Assembly Park once more.

Silver lake and giant forest
  Many hours like this recall,
While they sing with tuneful measure:
  Happy greetings one and all!

Are we all at our Round Table?
  All who gathered years ago?
No, some tender links are broken,
  And our tears awhile must flow.

Far beyond the silent river,
  Some have laid their burdens down;
They have heard the Savior's welcome,
  And received their promised crown.

Now they bid us weep no longer,
  But enjoy the pleasant hours,
Till by angels we are wafted
  To their paradise of flowers.

Hail, Chautauquan sons and daughters,
  Nature joins our song of love;
Happy greeting, happy greeting,
  To our temple in the grove.

Good-night! Good-night!

On the last night of the old year, nineteen hundred
and five, I attended the watch-night services at the

First Methodist Episcopal Church in Bridgeport. I had previously prepared a poem entitled "The Message of the Old Year" which I recited there, and with this I, too, will bid you all "good-night."

List to the clanging bells of time,
Tolling, tolling a low, sad chime,
A requiem chant o'er the grand Old Year,
Hark! he is speaking, and bids us hear:

"Friends, I am dying, my hours are few,
This is the message I leave for you—
Bought with a price, ye are not your own,
Live for the Master and him alone.

"Gather the sheep from the mountains cold,
Gather them into the Shepherd's fold,
Work for his cause till your work is done,
Stand by the cross till your crown is won.

"Epworth League, there are hosts above
Watching your labor of zeal and love,
Faithful abide till your days are past,
Then what a joy will be yours at last.

"I shall be gone ere the newborn year
Comes in its beauty the world to cheer:
Once I was young, and my flowers were bright—
Think of me kindly. Good-night! Good-night!"